MW00476042

KEN&Thelma

KEN&Thelma

The Story of
A Confederacy of Dunces

By Joel L. Fletcher

PELICAN PUBLISHING COMPANY
Gretna 2005

For J. A. C.

Library of Congress Cataloging-in-Publication Data

Fletcher, Joel L.
  Ken and Thelma : the story of A confederacy of dunces / by Joel L. Fletcher.
    p. cm.
  Includes bibliographical references and index.
  ISBN 9781589802964 (alk. paper)
  1. Toole, John Kennedy, 1937-1969. Confederacy of dunces. 2. Novelists,
American—20th century—Biography. 3. Mothers and sons—Louisiana—New
Orleans. 4. Toole, John Kennedy, 1937-1969—Estate. 5. New Orleans (La.)—
Intellectual life. 6. New Orleans (La.)—Biography. 7. Toole, Thelma. I. Title.

  PS3570.O54C6634 2005
  813'.54—dc22

                              2004024786

Printed in the United States of America

Published by Pelican Publishing Company, Inc.
1000 Burmaster Street, Gretna, Louisiana 70053

Table of Contents

ACKNOWLEDGMENTS

This book would never have been written without the urging and encouragement of John Copenhaver and Amos and Vaughan Simpson, who were persistent in their insistence that I write it. James D. Houston read an early version of my manuscript and made suggestions that put me on the right track. Cornelia Montgomery served as my perceptive first editor on the Nantucket ferry. Jane Bonin and S. Frederick Starr were both enormously helpful. A number of other people, generous with time, information, and wise advice, also played an important role in its creation. They include:

William Clark
Clayelle Dalferes
Ann Dobie
Kenneth Holditch
David Kubach
Gary Libby
Stephen S. Lottridge

Welton P. Mouton, Jr
Nicholas Polites
Patricia Rickels
Dr. Patricia Romano
Carl Selph
Ethel Chachere Simpson
David Swoyer

I would like to thank Robert Gottlieb for giving me permission to quote from his correspondence, Carmine

Palumbo for letting me quote from his interview with Bobby Byrne, Jackie Brenner, and Philip Gould for permission to reproduce their superb photographs. I would also like to thank Wilbur E. Meneray and Leon C. Miller of Tulane University for their making it so easy to consult the Toole archive, and Bruce Turner of the University of Louisiana at Lafayette for finding the photograph of the USL English faculty that includes so many of the people who appear in this book.

INTRODUCTION

The story of *A Confederacy of Dunces* is a remarkable one of how a celebrated and much-loved novel was almost lost, and then miraculously saved. It is the story of the gifted writer who created it and then died young, thinking his life had been a failure. It is also the story of his mother, an indomitable force who overcame enormous grief, illness, and profound disappointment with her own life to get the novel published, and who then lived long enough to see it become a huge success, to win the Pulitzer Prize, to stake its claim as a classic of American literature.

A greatly simplified and distorted version of the story has long been known to the reading public. Some of this version, of course, is true, but it is basically the story as told by the author's mother and energetically promoted by her, and it ignores much of what is really interesting about the history of the book. There were aspects of the story that Thelma Toole did not want known, and, in her grief, probably could not face.

It was my good fortune to have known Ken Toole while he was working on *A Confederacy of Dunces,* to have written in my journal about him at the time, and to have saved the letters he wrote to me, which provide insight both into his life and his work. By chance, I also knew quite well Bobby Byrne, the real-life eccentric who was the inspiration for the hero of the book, the bizarre Ignatius Reilly. And, perhaps most importantly, after the author's death, I got to know and closely observe Thelma, his formidable mother, without whom *A Confederacy of Dunces* would never have seen the light of day.

Re-reading the following pages after I had written them, I realized that in my book, as in life, Ken is dominated by the overwhelming presence of his mother. Perhaps it should be called *Thelma and Ken,* instead of the other way around. Ken's wit and intelligence are certainly there, best expressed in his letters, but somehow Ken himself remains at a distance. He was an acute observer, but did not let himself be easily observed. He was by nature reticent and elusive, and too soon eluded the world altogether by his suicide.

My most vivid memory of Ken is of his wry smile when he was telling an amusing story or witnessing an absurdity. Finally, like the Cheshire cat, the smile is all that is left. And then his mother takes the stage.

There is undoubtedly more that may be discovered about the story of *Confederacy,* much that remains unwritten, and perhaps one day will be, but the account that follows came mostly from what I, as a witness, saw and heard and learned first hand. This is a memoir, not a biography. A good biography of John Kennedy Toole is yet to be written. I hope that a future biographer of Toole will find this account a useful and accurate document. I also hope it casts much light on the most important relationship of the writer's life: that with his mother, Thelma Ducoing Toole.

KEN&Thelma

CHAPTER ONE

Ken

In a journal I kept during the summer of 1960, I wrote about a new friend: John Kennedy Toole (Ken, to his friends). We were both in Lafayette, Louisiana, for the summer. I had grown up there and my father was the president of the University of Southwestern Louisiana, where Ken had been teaching for the past year. A mutual friend, Nicholas Polites, who was then living in Chicago, suggested that we meet. Ken was finishing his last semester at USL before returning to graduate work at Columbia. In an act of unashamed nepotism, my father had found me a summer job writing press releases for the USL news bureau before I returned to graduate work at Stanford. Neither of us was very happy to be spending a hot, muggy, bug-ridden summer in dusty (when it wasn't pouring with rain) Lafayette.

About the time we met, Ken began working on the novel that would bring him posthumous fame and glory: *A Confederacy of Dunces.* It was published twelve years after his death and won a Pulitzer Prize. Unlike many prize-winning novels, it has proved extremely durable. Critics have pointed out its flaws, but its flaws are irrelevant to those who love the book, and they are legion. It has sold more than a million and a half copies, been published in eighteen languages, and is still selling briskly and finding new admirers today. Many consider it the best novel ever written about New Orleans, and a large part of its magic lies in the way Ken captured the particular flavor and the eccentric character of that city.

As Kenneth Holditch has pointed out in his essay *Another Kind of Confederacy,* Ken was "as irrevocably tied to New Orleans as Faulkner *was* to Oxford, Mississippi. No other writer, native or otherwise, seems to have *known* the city as well nor to have been able to evoke its sights and sounds and smells as powerfully as he." And yet the novel obviously has a universal appeal that transcends the local color so accurately captured by Ken. How else to account for its worldwide success?

I don't recall precisely the first time I saw Ken. At the time I was working in the musty basement of a campus administration building at USL. I believe Ken must have showed up there one day and introduced himself.

The first mention of Ken in my diary is on July 10. A passage describes a weekend trip to New Orleans. I had given Ken a ride home on Friday afternoon, and we had met for lunch the next day at my favorite bar in the French Quarter, the Napoleon House. After beers and a sandwich, we spent much of the afternoon browsing through bookstores. I was looking for books about Louisiana for my father, who collected them. We went to what were then the best bookstores in the Quarter: the Plantation, Coronet, and the Southern Bookmart. In one of them we had an

unexpected encounter with a famous Southern novelist. As
we were walking out the door, the clerk, pointing toward
an immense spread of female derrière thrust upward while
its owner searched for a book on a bottom shelf, whispered
to us: "*That* is Frances Parkinson Keyes!"

Of the rest of the afternoon I wrote in my journal:

> We walked through the Quarter to Elysian Fields, now
> a totally decayed neighborhood where all the doors
> have shutters, and all the shutters are cracked open
> only at eye level—people standing in doorways—old
> couples sitting on their doorsteps. Dirty-looking
> mothers screaming at their much dirtier children.
> Suddenly, we were caught in a shower of large, thun-
> dering raindrops. "GET IN OUTTA DAT RAIN,
> CHA'LIE!" one of the mothers yelled at her child, and
> (WHAP!) struck the child with a convenient board.
> "GET IN OUTTA DAT RAIN! YOU'LL GET SICK!"
> (WHAP!) She struck again. Ken was transfixed by the
> scene. Soaked, we walked to the docks below the
> Quarter and stood in the doorway of an enormous steel
> warehouse where we looked 'across the harbor wet
> with rain,' the wide, muddy Mississippi. When the
> rain stopped, we followed the railroad tracks to the
> French Market where black men were unloading
> trucks of watermelons, pitching them off underhand
> and counting out 'fohty-fo, fohty-five, fohty-six.' We
> stopped at the Morning Call Café and over *café au lait*
> with chicory, Ken mimicked the Elysian Fields moth-
> er braining her child while voicing such concern over
> his welfare, chuckling to himself, delighted by the
> comic irony.

Years later, when I read *Confederacy* for the first time, I thought of poor "Cha'lie" and his mom when I read Ken's description in *Confederacy* of Santa Battaglia abusing her grandchildren: "Get away from that stove, Charmaine, and go play on the banquette before I bust you right in the mouth." We had seen Santa Battaglia on Elysian Fields.

I noted in my journal of the summer of 1960: "Ken has a real gift for mimicry and a refined sense of the absurd . . . the English faculty at USL, which is divided into several camps of war, both fear and court Ken because of his biting comic talent."

We spent a good bit of time together that summer. Often we drove out of Lafayette on sultry evenings and drank beer in country bars. We discovered that we shared a few literary enthusiasms, the chief among them the comic novels of Evelyn Waugh and Flannery O'Connor's short stories and novellas. Ken was mad for the husky-voiced jazz singer Frances Faye "Is Frances Faye God?" he would sometimes ask. Of course, we never found her records on the jukeboxes of the Cajun bars around Lafayette.

I was a new face and a new ear for Ken to fill with his impressions of his English department colleagues. It was from Ken that I first heard about Bobby Byrne, the eccentric New Orleanian who taught English with him and was indisputably the inspiration for Ignatius J. Reilly, the main character in *A Confederacy of Dunces.*

As described by Walker Percy in his foreword to *Confederacy,* Ignatius is "a slob extraordinary . . . in violent revolt against the entire modern age." That is a somewhat exaggerated, but fairly accurate description of Byrne.

I met Bobby the same summer I met Ken. The next year, when I unexpectedly joined the English faculty of USL to replace an instructor who at the last minute decided not to accept his appointment, I got to know him somewhat better. He was hard to miss. One of our colleagues remarked that Lafayette was a poor venue for Bobby's monumental eccentricity and that he really should have been at some place like Harvard where his peculiarities would have been more appreciated. Bobby was a large man with curly black hair and a nose that looked as if it might have been broken in a brawl, though undoubtedly it hadn't been. His appearance and manner intimidated some of his students. He could look fearsome and acted gruff at times, but he was basically a gentle soul.

Bobby and Ken had grown up in the same uptown New Orleans neighborhood. Bobby did not meet Ken until they were both on the English faculty at Southwestern, but he was aware of the Toole family earlier because his Aunt May had taught Ken in grammar school. Thelma Toole, Ken's formidable mother, and her "genius son" had sometimes been a topic of conversation in the Byrne household. In an interview that Bobby gave in 1995 to Carmine Palumbo, a graduate student at USL, he mentioned that his aunt had liked Ken very much, but had been less than enthusiastic about his mother. "Thelma Toole gives me the pip!" Bobby quoted her as saying. Every so often his aunt would run into Thelma, and later say: "Well, I saw Thelma Toole today, and she's still Thelma Toole."

Before coming to Lafayette in 1958, Bobby, who was a decade older than Ken, had taught at both Tulane in New Orleans and Louisiana State University in Baton Rouge.

But when he began to teach at Southwestern, he seemed to find his niche and remained in Lafayette for the rest of his life. He lived for many years in a small cottage and a room attached to a garage behind the home of Ralph Lynch, another member of the English faculty. It was within walking distance of the campus. He lived a rather solitary life with stacks of books and journals and sheet music and a harpsichord he played very badly. He traveled little, except for regular trips back to his New Orleans home during school vacations. The only major excursions he made were several to the *Eisteddfod,* the music and literary festival held each summer in Wales. The week-long festival, which promotes Welsh music, literature, language, and customs, is a gathering of bards who compete among themselves for honors. I do not know if Bobby took part in these competitions. He was a performing musician of sorts, but very likely at the *Eisteddfod* he was only an observer. On these trips he was careful to choose flights that took him directly to Wales without having layovers in London, which he considered a center of decadence.

One of Bobby's students, Ken had told me, never took notes on Bobby's lectures, but instead filled her notebook with detailed lists of the bizarre combinations of clothes and accessories he wore to class each day. Once Bobby had appeared at the small office in the English department which he and Ken shared wearing three different kinds of plaid and an absurd hat. "My God, Bobby!" Ken reported that he had exclaimed. "You look like the April Fool cover of *Esquire*!"

James Lee Burke, the noted mystery writer who was briefly part of the USL English faculty, also once shared an office with Bobby. He told me that one day he passed the open door of a classroom in which sat a collection of hunched and sprawled freshmen. It was a section of remedial English being taught by Bobby, who was jumping up and down energetically and gesticulating wildly while drawing large circles on the blackboard. The students, Jim said, looked stunned and fearful. When Bobby returned to the office, Jim asked, "For God's sake, Bobby, what were you teaching those poor kids? Dante?" "Of course not!" Bobby replied haughtily. "Prepositions."

I remember that one day as I was walking across the campus with Bobby, I began to whistle a piece of music that was going through my mind.

"What's that you're whistling?" Bobby demanded.

"I think it's the *scherzo* from a Beethoven quartet," I replied.

"I've always resented *scherzi,*" said Bobby. "They replaced the minuet, you know."

"It is likely that I reported this exchange to Ken. I knew it was the kind of anecdote he would have found amusing. I remembered it when I read the passage in Confederacy in which Ignatius enters Paradise Vendors, Incorporated, and purchases a hot dog from the old man who is boiling them in "a large institutional pot." While he is chewing the dog with "a blissful savagery," he listens to the man whistling:

> "Do I hear a strain from Scarlatti?" Ignatius asked finally.
>
> "I thought I was whistling Turkey in the Straw."
>
> "I had hoped you might be familiar with Scarlatti's work. He was the last of the musicians."

There have been a few other claimants to the title of inspiration for Ignatius, but no one, not even Bobby himself, has ever disputed that he was Ken's model.

I had known some of Ken's other colleagues, of course, since my days as a campus brat. Muriel McCullough Price, senior member of the English Department, was one of those. Muriel had been born in the little town of Thibodeaux on the Bayou Lafourche, but one would never have guessed it from her accent. I wrote in my journal of an evening Ken and I spent with Muriel and several others in her book-filled apartment: "Muriel . . . is imperturbable and caustic. She cherishes the broad 'a' and it grows broader with each highball." Hearing her remarkable accent, someone had once asked J.C. Broussard, one of her colleagues and also a friend of Ken's, where she was from. "Thibodeaux, England," he replied.

On the evening in question, Ken and I were served the highballs that Muriel cherished as much as her broad "a" and listened to her hold forth on the idiocies of contemporary life: "Seven-thirty claahses are ab-so-lute-ly baahrbaric!" And the splendors of the past. Especially the Romantic period in English literature, in which she fancied herself a specialist, though Ken expressed a suspicion that she had probably not read nor seriously thought about the Romantic poets she taught for at least thirty years, anticipating Dr. Talc in *Confederacy* who "was renowned for the facile and sarcastic wit and easily digested generalizations that . . . helped to conceal his lack of knowledge about almost everything in general and British history in particular."

During that long ago summer, Ken was living in a dank

garage apartment on Convent Street (the same street that
Katherine Ann Porter had lived on during her sojourn in
Lafayette many years before). The apartment belonged to
and was behind the home of Elisabeth Montgomery, one of
the pillars of local society. Mrs. Montgomery was then a
hyperactive widow in her sixties, one of Lafayette's great
"costume pieces." She loved pink and she loved red, and she
often wore them together in striking combination: a pink
pinafore, red high heels, a pink camellia pinned in her hair.
She dressed the way she must have dressed when she had
been a sweet, young Southern girl of eighteen. Hers was a
honeyed but shrill voice for preserving the status quo of the
social structure of the Old South, and she was alarmed by
the body blows it recently had been receiving. She was,
however, a rapt admirer of the incipient oil boom and the
wealth it had begun to bring to Lafayette, and an early sup-
porter of the burgeoning Republican Party in Louisiana.
She lived for the local Mardi Gras, which, with the influx
of Texas oil money, had begun to rival in excess the older
and more extensive revelries in New Orleans.

Elisabeth often told the story of how once when she was
a young girl visiting relatives on a plantation in
Mississippi, one of her cousins was making "cherry
bounce." A kind of southern cordial, cherry bounce is made
by soaking wild cherries in bourbon for six months. The
cherries are then discarded and a simple syrup is added to
the bourbon. The resulting potent drink is sometimes
served over ice cream or sipped from liqueur glasses.
During Elisabeth's visit, her cousin had thrown out the
bourbon-soaked cherries and his flock of turkeys had found

them, eaten them, got drunk, and all passed out. The cook, seeing the turkeys lying inert on the ground, thought they had died and decided that the best thing to do was to pluck them and cook them before they spoiled. According to Elisabeth, as the cook got the last feather off the last turkey, they began to come to. It was November and getting cold in the Delta, and the naked turkeys were looking very uncomfortable. "Ah knew just what to do," said Elisabeth. "Ah went into town and bought yards and yards of pink flannel and ah made 'em all pinafores!"

Ken found this superannuated Southern belle amusing. He was less amused by the depressing furnished apartment where he spent too many hours alone. I don't recall ever seeing the inside of the apartment—perhaps we had coffee together there once—but I do remember him describing it in Conradian metaphor: a cramped heart of darkness with cockroaches and a linoleum floor, made even darker by Mrs. Montgomery's frequent admonitions, since utilities were included in the rent, to keep the outside light turned off.

One August evening my parents gave a dinner party and invited Ken and his landlady. Mrs. Montgomery had just returned from a trip to Alaska where she had ridden in a dog sled and eaten raw blubber. "Some peoh-ple bawl it, ya'know. But thay-et's sooo nahhsty! Eskimos ahhr the naihsest peoh-ple! Why, whenehvah thehre's ahny trouh-ble, thehre's *ahlways* a whaite mahn b'hind it!"

This was the first time that Ken had socialized with his landlady. He was clearly intrigued by the extravagances of this living caricature of the Old South, and had he lived to write more fiction, I would not have been surprised had she appeared in it thinly disguised, much as Bobby had appeared so recognizably in *Confederacy.*

Among the other guests that evening were a Mr. and Mrs. Crump. I don't remember anything about Mr. Crump, but his wife was unforgettable. She always wore lots of make-up and very long false eyelashes. (She had once lost an eyelash at a cocktail party, then spotting it on the floor and mistaking it for a cockroach, had screamed and tried to stomp it to death.) That evening Mrs. Crump was dressed in a low-cut, white dress with a wide red sash. "She dresses like what she's *not,*" my mother charitably said of her.

"Her necklace was a ghastly thing," I noted in my diary, "of great glass balls in sufficient quantity to buoy a Japanese fishing net. Her conversation was a series of exclamations aimed at different guests."

Mrs. Crump was a published (at her husband's expense) poetess (the term she probably would have used), but the conversation that evening never took a literary turn. Ken was seated between Mrs. Montgomery and Mrs. Crump. I was directly across from him. He said little, nor did anyone but Mrs. Montgomery and Mrs. Crump, who verbally dueled for the floor.

The food was good, as it usually is in southern Louisiana, the evening did not go on so long as to become tedious, and Ken seemed amused at the small menagerie my mother had assembled at her table. My most vivid memory of Ken that evening is an expression of silent glee on his face when Mrs. Crump, absorbed in a point she was making to my father, took a bowl of sugar Ken was passing to her. Not realizing that his finger was still in the handle, she tugged at it vigorously, never taking her eyes off my father. Ken, a smile on his lips, looked up to see if I were a witness to her determined struggle with his finger.

A few days later, classes over, Ken departed Lafayette to spend what was left of the summer in New Orleans. By September, I was back in California and Ken was back in New York.

Ken had first gone to New York as a teenager on a school trip in May of 1954. His scrapbook of the trip documents what seems to have been an exhilarating experience. According to the bits and pieces in the scrap book, Ken took the train, *The Southerner,* with other students to New York, Philadelphia, and Washington, D.C., the final destination, where the group was awarded the "Freedom Foundation Award for its presentation of democratic practices in the school life of Alcee Fortier Senior High School." The visit to New York is given the most space in the album, and seems to have been the highlight of the trip.

His time in New York is documented with photographs of a rather pudgy Ken on an excursion boat in New York harbor, in Chinatown, at the Statue of Liberty, in Times Square. There are programs from Radio City Music Hall where he saw the Rockettes and the movie *Executive Suite* with June Allyson, and the Winter Garden Theater where he saw *Wonderful Town* with Carol Channing.

New York must have made a big impression on Ken because the scrapbook also documents another trip he made to New York the following September with his Fortier friend Stephen Andry. A photograph shows him in a Pontiac convertible in which he and Stephen made the trip.

Mementoes of this visit include programs from the NBC Century Theater featuring *Coke Time* with Eddie Fisher and the Vaughan Monroe Show. There is also a program of the production *Cat on a Hot Tin Roof* with Burl Ives as "Big Daddy." Perhaps his early experiences of New York were a factor in his decision to choose Columbia University for his graduate study. He first enrolled there in the autumn of 1958 after winning a Woodrow Wilson Fellowship.

In the autumn of 1960, Ken was back in New York, after a year of teaching in Lafayette, living in "a room on Riverside Drive that is large and bright, has a limited view of the Hudson and New Jersey across the river, and is inexpensive by New York standards," he wrote in a letter to his Uncle Arthur and Aunt "Nandy" in New Orleans.

In a letter to his parents written about the same time, he described his life in New York:

> Every morning here at Hunter on Park teaching; in the afternoon I make it across town to Columbia to take courses. Hunter is a sixteen-story building constructed along the lines of Charity Hospital in New Orleans. They both have in common that institutionalized aspect of public buildings of the 1930s.

It is telling that Ken compares the building at Hunter where he was teaching to the Charity Hospital in New Orleans. In the last chapter of *Confederacy,* Irene and Santa Battaglia plot to send Ignatius to the psychiatric ward of the New Orleans Charity Hospital. Ken seems to have been inspired by the last scene of another great literary work set in New Orleans: *A Street Car Named Desire,* in which a doctor and nurse come to take Blanche Dubois off to a mental hospital. The last scene of *Confederacy* is almost a parody of it. But Ignatius is presumably luckier than Blanche. Blanche, just before she is committed, is expecting her former beau Shep Huntleigh to call for her. Ignatius is rescued by his old girl friend, the unexpected Myrna Minkoff, with her pigtail and guitar, who suddenly appears, a drab and earnest *deus ex machina,* to take him off to New York City, beating the ambulance from Charity by seconds.

Ken and Thelma, as will be seen later, had some experience of a family member being sent to the psychiatric ward at Charity.

That winter Ken wrote me that he was unhappy with his Ph.D. studies at Columbia, but that he liked Hunter, where he was teaching, "principally because the aggressive, pseudo-intellectual, 'liberal' girl students are continuously amusing." Myrna Minkoff, the unlikely heroine of *Confederacy* was under observation. In a letter to his parents, he elaborated: "The students here are for the most part very sharp, very eager and interested, very worthwhile. The all-girl student body is principally Jewish and Irish, balanced in about a 50-50 split, and all drawn from the New York Metropolitan area."

In the letter to me, Ken mentioned the recent presidential election. "At this early date it looks as if Kennedy may justify my faith in him, although I'm only very grateful that we were spared Dick and Pat. What a disappointment the election must have been to Mrs. Montgomery."

In the autumn of 1962 I found a teaching job in Italy and settled in Florence for what was supposed to have been one year, but turned into five. Ken had been drafted into the army and was teaching recruits in Puerto Rico. In late September I received the first letter from San Juan:

> We are all rotting here at the moment. The decreased draft has meant no trainees since June; therefore, there is no English to teach, and cobwebs and mold are beginning to overtake the SPEAK ENGLISH signs posted throughout the Training Center. I am now in charge of the English program here . . . a hollow position for the nonce. The benefits of the position are two-fold: supervision rather than teaching; a bright, comfortable, airy private room. The inactivity here, coupled with the remnants of a rainy and enervating summer, has (have?) plunged the English instructors into an abyss of drinking and inertia. Occasionally someone will struggle off to the beach or to San Juan, but the maxim here remains, 'It's too hot.' Cafard, Bobby Byrne's nemesis, has struck.

Ken must have soon overcome the inertia of which he wrote for it was in the "bright, comfortable, airy private room" that he began to revise an earlier novel and transform it into *Confederacy*.

About two months later, I received a second letter from Ken. It sounded as if he were absorbed in and amused by his army life in Puerto Rico:

> The arrival of the trainees in late October has kept me very busy; as the "dean" of the English program here, I am lost in test scores and averages and in the maze of painfully intricate Army politics and intrigue. I am quite powerful in my own little way and exercise more

control over personnel and affairs in general than I had ever suspected I would; over my private telephone I contact headquarters, switching people here and there, waiting, listening, planning. I'm sure I will leave my duty here a completely mad tyrant whose niche in civilian life will be non-existent. In its own lunatic way, this is very entertaining . . . After a year in Puerto Rico (as of 25 Nov), I find that the positive aspects of that year outweigh the negative. Although this seems a great cliché, I can say that I have learned a vast amount about humans and their natures—information which I would have enjoyed having earlier. In my own curious way I have risen "meteorically" in the Army without having ever been a decent prospect for military life; but I feel that my very peculiar assignment has been responsible. The insanity and unreality of Puerto Rico itself has been interesting at all times that it was not overwhelming. (great agreement errors in this sentence, I fear). Please write. Ken

I heard from Ken again at the end of January. He had been back in New Orleans on leave for the Christmas holidays:

Physically, New Orleans looked wonderful, as it always does. It is certainly one of the most beautiful cities in the world, although how the people who live there managed to make it so remains a mystery to me . . . I . . . paid the ritualistic visits to the Byrne home (coffee, Aunt May, Mama, et al) where, of course, little has changed but the pot of fresh coffee and chicory. Bobby's worldview weathers humanity's derision and apathy. He does, however, begin to appear old. Both he and his brother received holiday visitors in long nightshirts and slippers with rather haughty formality, and Bobby was, as always, good for a dogma or two.

Ken had also had spent time with some of our mutual friends in the Sazerac Bar of the Roosevelt (now the Fairmont) Hotel. The group included Nicholas Polites and J. C. Broussard.

Each of them went home and wrote me a letter describing the afternoon in the bar, and the three letters, which I dubbed "The Roosevelt Hotel triptych," all arrived on the same day in Florence. Ken's letter (see appendix) was the wickedest and funniest of the three. In a passage in which there seems to hover the spirit of Patrolman Mancuso, who tries to arrest Ignatius in the opening pages of *Confederacy,* Ken wrote: "We must have appeared a dubious group in the bar, and I'm afraid that I made my departure rather rapidly . . . before the house detective took us all away."

In an undated letter, though it must have been written in the autumn of 1963, Ken wrote from New Orleans:

I left Puerto Rico in August. The two years in the Caribbean were, surprisingly, worthwhile from several points of view. I at least completed the active military obligation, and the Army treated me well (remember that we are speaking here in the context of military treatment) and gave me the leisure to accomplish several projects of my own. Puerto Rico itself was worth experiencing: one can appreciate Conrad much more deeply after having lived there for two years. [Ken had told me much the same thing about Mrs. Montgomery's garage apartment in Lafayette, and Ignatius in *Confederacy* imagines himself as Kurtz in *The Heart of Darkness* when he visits the Levy pants factory.]

For now I have sought temporary shelter in New Orleans by teaching at Dominican College for the 1963-64 academic year. Because I teach only 10½ hours a week, I still seem to have the same leisure I enjoyed in the Army. The college has been in session for about two weeks, and so far the routine there has been extremely pleasant. Barring some inquisition, I should have a serene year, and with the salary they've given me, a very financially solvent one, also . . .

Aside from a brief visit with B. Byrne toward the end of the summer, I have had no connections with the Lafayette axis. According to Bobby, a meeting concerning textbooks held for the members of the English dept. late last Spring ended very badly indeed. Although he would not elaborate, he hinted that the meeting was climaxed by insults and near-violence . . . Bobby was still (and this was late August) extremely upset.

The next summer I was in Louisiana for a few weeks after several years of living abroad, and I must have been unbearably full of the experience. Ken had settled into his teaching at Dominican, and Bobby Byrne was in New Orleans for the summer break. We met one night for drinks at the Napoleon House, where the same scratchy records of classical music which had been played there when I was a student at Tulane almost a decade before were still to be heard on the phonograph. We sat on the patio, where the music was not so loud, sipped our drinks, and talked for several hours. I had been sure that both Bobby and Ken would be fascinated to hear all about my life abroad, and was very disappointed to discover that all they seemed to want to do was gossip about their uptown New Orleans neighborhood. I finally gave up trying to tell them about the marvelous things I had seen and done in Europe, drank my whisky, and smugly thought how provincial they seemed now that I had become a citizen of "the greater world!"

In May of 1965, back in Florence, I received another letter from Ken. It was addressed to me and to Nicholas Polites, the mutual friend who had suggested we meet that summer in Lafayette. Nicholas had been spending a year traveling around Europe, using my apartment in Florence as a base.

> Since both of you know of my writing project, I must say that eight air mail letters and one hour-long long distance call from Simon and Schuster later, I am still faced with revisions. Although I am "wildly funny often, funnier than almost anyone else around," the book is too 'intelligent to be only a farce.' It must have 'purpose and meaning.' However, it is full of 'wonderfulnesses' and 'excitements' and 'glories.'
>
> But they worked 'more than three years on *Catch-22.*' If and when it does appear, it will be unbearably 'significant,' I imagine. Also, I am like 'one of those geniuses who turn up in Tanganyika or New Zealand.' Poor New Orleans. Suppose I had sent the thing in from Breaux Bridge . . . or Parks. [small, and even smaller, towns in southern Louisiana] Broken and leering toothlessly, I may yet be on some book jacket. Looking at this more

constructively, I have been (and am) fortunate in having
the book reach so quickly people who have responded to
it and who have, by their response, given me a degree of
confidence in what I'm trying to do; goodness knows
they've extended much time and interest.

If I received other letters from Ken, they have been lost.
The ones I quoted from turned up in a suitcase I had left in
Florence in 1967 and retrieved in the 1980s. I think our
correspondence must have dwindled as I became much
busier than I had been when a friend and I quixotically
bought a failing language school in Florence and set out to
revitalize it. It was the sixties and not a few young people
were following unconventional paths; while many of my
contemporaries were experimenting with substances that
had to be inhaled or ingested, I had decided that Italy was
my drug of choice, and I was looking for a viable and interesting way to remain there. I had a great deal to write
about, but not much time for writing. Ken had heard about
the language school, a very modest venture, from Viva
Periou, one of Bobby's students with whom he had become
friendly. My father had generously advanced me a small
sum to buy my half interest in this establishment, which
consisted of about fifty prospective students, a stack of used
textbooks, several rooms of used furniture, and a short lease
on a rented apartment. In his last letter to me Ken wrote:

Viva said that she had heard that "Mr. Fletcher bought
Joel a college in Florence!" She was impressed—and,
of course, I was. In an epoch in which Ford Mustangs
and portable TV sets pass as gifts, a college is indeed a

particularly large but also recherché gift. Bobby Byrne, who has been wanting a college of his own for many years, did not mention this to me the last time that I saw him. I suspect envy as the motivation for his silence. And in Florence, with the ghosts of the Guelphs and Ghibellines hovering, Bobby would be driven to new heights of teaching excellence.

I was in Florence for the flood in 1966. Our little school survived this disaster, and even grew, but a year or so later I was offered an interesting job in Paris and took it, just in time for a front row seat for the *événements* of 1968. I was living in Paris when Ken took his life in the Gulf Coast town of Biloxi in March of 1969. He had written in the last letter I had from him, just after the paragraph about his dealings with Simon and Schuster:

> All of which leads to something else, I guess. The Gulf Coast looks better when you're not there. I was there recently; it looked much more appealing in under-graduate days.

I am sure I found nothing unusual in the juxtaposition of these two paragraphs when I first received the letter, but re-reading the letter with the knowledge that he was to commit suicide a few years later in Biloxi, it strikes a strange note. Why should what he wrote about his efforts to finish *Confederacy* and get it published lead "to some-thing else . . . the Gulf Coast . . . which looks better when you're not there." Was he, on some level, already considering the idea of suicide in Biloxi, or am I reading too much into a casual remark? Perhaps not. Ken's friend, David Kubach, who was in the army with Ken in Puerto Rico, told me that when he was visiting Ken in New Orleans a few years before his suicide, they had driven one day to Biloxi and Ken had shown him the very place where he was to take his life. It was an unremarkable spot, and David wondered why Ken had shown it to him. He now feels that perhaps the plan had been incubating as a possibility in Ken's mind for a long time.

During the years after our correspondence ceased, I had news of Ken from other sources. J.C. Broussard wrote after Ken had returned to New Orleans from Puerto Rico:

> Ken came for two days at Christmas and, under the influence, confided in me his deplorable state—a virtu-al incarceration (*entre nous*) with parents prematurely senile and giving full vent to a latent possessiveness. My advice to him, who is too young for such, was to escape after this year.

Nick Polites, our mutual friend in Chicago, who by then had moved to New York, complained that on his visits to his parents in New Orleans he found it increasingly difficult to get in touch with Ken. "His mother always answers the phone. She says that she'll give him the message, but he never returns my call. I'm beginning to think that she never tells him I've phoned. She's building a wall around him!"

I was not a witness to the despair and paranoia that gradually claimed Ken after his return to New Orleans. I heard about it only much later, long after his death. Friends who saw him during these years have written that after Robert Gottlieb, the editor at Simon and Schuster who initially had been enthusiastic about Ken's manuscript, lost interest in the book and encouraged Ken to go on to some other project, Ken seems to have stopped writing. For the next three years he continued to teach English at Dominican College and study part-time toward his Ph.D. in English at Tulane.

The pressures on him at home must have increased as he became, for all practical purposes, the sole support of his retired father and his mother, who was finding it increasingly difficult to find employment as a teacher of elocution and presenter of school pageants, the two occupations with which she had supplemented her husband's meager income throughout their long marriage.

Gary Libby, now a museum director in Florida, remembers Ken vividly from a graduate class they took together at Tulane in 1968. The class was Anglo-Saxon literature, taught by Professor Huling Ussery, a demanding, pedantic scholar who was an authority on both Anglo-Saxon literature and the western novels of Louis L'Amour. It was the height of the "hippie revolution" and Libby remembers Ken well because of his attire and appearance, which contrasted greatly with the long hair, mustaches, tie-dyed T-shirts, and bell-bottom trousers worn by most of his fellow students. Every day Ken wore exactly the same outfit to class, as if it were a uniform: a stiffly starched white dress shirt, open at the neck, with the sleeves rolled up two turns; neatly pressed black slacks; and a pair of highly polished black shoes. His hair was always carefully groomed, slicked down, and parted on the left. At first Libby thought that Ken might have been a waiter, a bow tie in his pocket, on his way to work. The class was a difficult one and Ken was the best student in it. He seemed to consider Anglo-Saxon child's play, Libby said. He also seemed older and more mature than the other students.

In the months before his suicide, Ken's appearance began to change. Ken, who had been compulsive about neatness, began to appear in public unshaved and uncombed, wearing unpolished shoes and wrinkled clothes, to the amazement of his friends and students in New Orleans. He had always had a fondness for alcohol. Most of the times I spent with Ken were over beer or whisky, and after a visit to Aruba, he had to written me: "The bar at the resort hotel deserves great praise." As his situation became more desperate, he probably began to drink more heavily.

He confided to some of his friends that people were plotting against him, that people were trying to steal his book, and that people were spying on him. One night over dinner, he told Patricia and Milton Rickels, his closest friends in Lafayette, that the wife of a former Southwestern colleague, who worked for Simon and Schuster in New York, was stealing the book for her husband. The husband was George Deaux, the novelist, who had taught briefly on the English faculty at Southwestern before publishing his first novel. Patricia, who initially believed the story, was horrified. Rick realized that Ken was delusional and later told Patricia, "Ken is losing his mind."

In his interview with Carmine Palumbo, Bobby Byrne spoke about the last time he saw Ken:

that dreadful session, which disturbed me a great deal, because he was obviously paranoid. I know enough about psychology to know paranoia when I see it; I've had enough paranoid friends to know when someone is paranoid, and he was. The girls [at Dominican] were whispering about him, people were writing nasty notes behind his back, people were driving by the house at all hours of the night honking their horns, and all sorts of things like that. He said, do you think I am imagining these things?

I said, yes Ken I do. I said you need to get some professional help. They say he did, but evidently it didn't take.

In 1970, the FDA approved the use of Lithium as a prescription drug to treat some of the very symptoms Ken was experiencing, but whatever professional help Ken sought, it was a year too soon for the drug that might have saved his life.

While he was in the army in Puerto Rico, Ken, in a letter to his parents, described the difficult first sergeant he was working under at Fort Buchanan: "His paranoid suspicion of humanity is overwhelming." By the autumn of 1968, his description of the sergeant fit his own state of mind. In November of that year, he stood up in one of his Tulane graduate courses and made a rambling speech accusing the faculty of conspiring to keep him from receiving his Ph.D. Suffering the pain, confusion, and terror caused by the onset of paranoia, suicide may well have already been on his mind.

Marilyn Monroe had been one of Ken's early passions. In the Toole archive at Tulane is a cartoon he drew for the *Hullabaloo,* the Tulane student newspaper. It appeared in

November of 1956, shortly after the release of the film *Bus Stop,* which starred Monroe. Ken had drawn a Marilyn look-alike leaning against the Freret Street bus stop at the Tulane campus. A passing coed says to another, "I don't know who she is, but she's been there for days!"

When he learned of her suicide in August of 1962, he wrote his parents from Puerto Rico: "In my own way I loved Marilyn Monroe very much. Marilyn Monroe made me happier (I can't think of another word) than any performer ever has. There was a time when my interest had reached the stage of obsession. Marilyn Monroe and death are such incongruous partners. It seems trite, I know, to say that I couldn't believe she was dead, but I couldn't. . . . A suicide who could find no bearings in the society which had formed her. Her life and death are both very sobering—and even frightening."

When classes resumed at Dominican after the Christmas break in January of 1969, Ken was missing. His mother thought that he was going to visit friends in Lafayette, but the friends he was supposed to be visiting never saw him. More than two months later, on March 26, Ken's body was discovered in his old Chevrolet in a wood near Biloxi, Mississippi.

He had purchased a length of garden hose, attached it to the exhaust pipe, and run it through the back window of the car. Receipts found by his body made it possible to piece together something about his last, sad odyssey. It appears that he went to California and visited San Simeon, the mansion of the Hearst family, then drove back east to Milledgeville, Georgia, the home of one of his late idols,

Flannery O'Connor. There was also an envelope addressed
to his parents that contained a suicide note. Thelma read it
and destroyed it. She later gave varying versions of what it
contained. "It asked me and my husband to forgive him for
what he had done and asked God to have mercy on his
soul," she sometimes said. But in unguarded moments, she
confided that it contained "insane ravings." Whatever Ken
wrote in his final note, Thelma has taken the truth of the
matter with her to the grave.

The first time I met the formidable Thelma Toole, and
the only time I saw her while her son was alive, was an
August afternoon in 1964. I had been back in Lafayette for
the summer, and was taking an Italian friend who had
spent a few days with me there to catch a plane in New
Orleans. Before we went to the airport, we stopped at the
Toole's pleasant and unpretentious duplex at 390 Audubon
Street, not far from Tulane University, and Mrs. Toole, with
theatrical flourish, served us lunch. Mr. Toole made a brief
appearance, dressed in a summer Boy Scout leader's uniform with short pants, and patted me and my Italian friend
enthusiastically on our knees. Ken seemed content enough.
He was apparently still very optimistic about the future of
his novel, which he was revising under the guidance of
Robert Gottlieb on an Olivetti portable he had purchased
for sixty-nine dollars at the PX in Puerto Rico. We ate
what Ken referred to as his mother's "famous stuffed tomatoes," and we must have talked about our mutual friends
and acquaintances. Except for meeting Ken's parents, the
visit was unremarkable. It was the last time I saw Ken.

Fifteen years later, living again in Lafayette, I read in the

New Orleans *Times-Picayune* an article about the imminent publication of *A Confederacy of Dunces.* It related the now-famous story of how Thelma had discovered Ken's manuscript, persisted in her attempts to find a publisher, and eventually persuaded Walker Percy to read the almost illegible typescript.

The *Times-Picayune* article contained a description of the house in which Mrs. Toole was then living with her brother on Elysian Fields Avenue, not far from where Ken and I years before had seen poor "Cha'lie" thrashed by his loving mom. A few weeks after the article appeared, I was in New Orleans to attend a meeting. I had breakfasted early with friends in the Faubourg Marigny and still had an hour or so to kill. I decided to drive down nearby Elysian Fields Avenue to see if I could find Mrs. Toole's house. From the description in the paper—a small, white cottage with a green awning, next to a funeral parlor, across from a Schwegmann's supermarket—it was easy to find. On impulse, I parked my car and went to the front door of the house. Through a dusty, diamond-shaped pane of glass, I could see a figure standing inside, a few feet away. I knocked and the figure moved slowly toward the door. It opened and there was Mrs. Toole standing in front of me, clutching her aluminum walker. "Mrs. Toole," I began to explain, "I doubt that you remember me, but I was a friend of Ken's. My name is Joel Fletcher. I just stopped by to tell you how glad I am that Ken's novel is going to be published."

"Come in, Joel, honey," she replied. "I was *just* thinking about you."

Chapter Two
Thelma

Mrs. Toole's greeting nearly brought up goose pimples on the back of my neck. It almost seemed as if she were expecting me, though she was hardly dressed for an occasion. She was wearing an old blue housedress and having difficulty getting around with a metal walker. In the small living room there were Venetian blinds on the windows, but no curtains, and the blinds were drawn shut. Most of the furniture in the room looked like vintage Sears, and the walls were of cheap faux-wood paneling. The linoleum on the floor was in an Oriental rug pattern. A small TV set was perched on an aluminum stand that resembled her aluminum walker.

She invited me to sit and indicated a pseudo-Victorian love seat behind a flimsy looking coffee table with cut glass baubles on it. Mrs. Toole sat in a wing chair next to the love seat and began to tell me the story of the book. She railed against Robert Gottlieb, the editor at Simon and Schuster, who rejected the novel after having given Ken so much encouragement. "A cruel man, a heartless man!" Her voice grew dark as she stressed each syllable. Then she told the happier story of how she had gotten Ken's novel published, how she had sent the manuscript to publisher after publisher and how it had always come back, until finally she had thrust it upon Walker Percy, who, after reading it, agreed with her assessment that it was a work of genius and eventually persuaded Louisiana State University Press to publish it.

She asked which of Ken's friends I knew, and mentioned several names that meant nothing to me. I told her that I had met Ken through Nick Polites, who had been a friend of Ken's at Tulane. "I remember Nicky," she said. "Ken thought he was very smart." Then she asked, "Did you know Doonie Guibet?" I told her that I had met him once. Doonie had at one time been Ken's closest friend, a handsome, somewhat effete blond, openly and obviously gay. Nick told me that Doonie had gone to New York where "he had lived on his wits, but not for very long!" In the 1960s I had met him briefly at Nick's family home on Arabella Street. He and Ken had come over while I was visiting Nick, and Nick's mother, Eugenia, had made us thick, black Turkish coffee, and read our fortunes in the grounds.

Mrs. Toole said that after Ken died, she called Doonie's mother to ask where Doonie was. "She was very curt and very crude and told me she didn't know where he was. I kept the letters that Doonie wrote Ken," Mrs. Toole said, though there are no letters from Doonie in the Tulane Library archive which received most of Ken's papers as a bequest from Thelma. A year later I made a chance discovery about Doonie, which I will describe later, and which perhaps explains why his letters to Ken were not included in Thelma's gift.

Mrs. Toole handed me a copy of the *New Orleans Review*

from a stack of them on the coffee table. "Take this, Joel, honey. It has a chapter of Ken's book. The book is coming out in about a month, according to Les Phillabaum, the head of LSU Press. Dear Walker. If it hadn't been for Walker!"

Mrs. Toole suggested that I might like to hear her play and sing some of the songs that Ken had loved. "My music is all I've had to get me through some very dark times." She rose and haltingly led the way into the dining room/kitchen that was dominated by a baby grand piano. "I bought this piano with money I made teaching school. It is my prize possession!" The piano was badly out of tune, and her playing was harsh and angry, as was her voice. She pounded rather than tickled the ivories and belted out the songs: *You're Nobody Till Somebody Loves You, Since You Went Away, I Cried For You, Who's Sorry Now.* Thelma made all the lyrics sound like heart-wrenching autobiography. One of the songs she sang was prophetic, and she sang it as if she knew it: *There'll be Some Changes Made.* The changes had already begun, first with Walker Percy, and then with the acceptance of *Confederacy* by LSU Press. Soon there would be many more changes in her life, most of them for the better. The lionization of Thelma had not yet begun, but when it did, I was to see much of it from close range, from the beginning to the end.

I believe that the key to understanding Ken, his achievement and his tragedy, lies in understanding Thelma. She was the force that shaped him, and, ultimately, a force that helped destroy him.

As I got to know Thelma better over the next few years, I found her fascinating, tiresome, engaging, and impossible.

She could both enhance life and stifle it. She was both generous and mean. Larger than life, she was an authentic *mon-
stre sacré.* She was her son's best friend and his worst enemy.
She was as much a tragic figure as he was, and I came to feel
a great compassion for her.

I was intrigued by Thelma, by who she was and how she
had become what she was. As I got to know her, I realized
that Thelma was the product of her family, the society in
which she had grown up, and her absorption in a theatrical
world that was partly of her own creation.

My friendship with Thelma began on that first visit to
her modest home on Elysian Fields Avenue. It was before
the publication of *Confederacy,* before the legend of the book
was spun for the public, before she emerged from obscurity to take her place in a spotlight she had craved from
childhood. Our friendship, which became more and more
difficult to maintain toward the end of her life, was probably prolonged by the Atchafalya Swamp that separated us.
If I had been closer to hand, she would have expected me to
be at her beck and call. That is what she had expected of
Ken, and, for a time, I was a kind of surrogate for him. She
knew, however, that she could not make the demands on
me that she had made on him, and the physical distance
between us helped me maintain the psychological distance
that was necessary to remain on friendly terms without
being overwhelmed by her. I was very fond of her, and very
grateful she was not *my* mother.

After the publication of *Confederacy,* her misery was alleviated
by its success and the commotion surrounding it. Thelma
emerged from her sadness to embrace that commotion

energetically, and for the remaining years of her life she devoted herself to furthering the fame of *Confederacy* and the memory of her "genius son." She also spent a great deal of time and energy promoting her version of why Ken had killed himself, controlling the legend of his death. She appeared on talk shows, went to book signings, and gave numerous public recitals in which she portrayed the various characters in her son's book.

As Thelma became increasingly visible, it became apparent how important she was in the formation of Ken as a writer. His great gift for observation and mimicry had obviously come from Thelma. When Ken was growing up, he and Thelma would amuse themselves by making up dialogues of what she referred to as "low-class New Orleans types." The voices he used in his games with Thelma became the voices of the characters in his novel. S. Frederick Starr, who was then vice-president of Tulane University, remembers sitting through one of her recitals at the Newcomb College chapel. "I felt that I was hearing Ken Toole in the raw, straight from the cask, and that he was the 'dumb' one who had the gift of being able to translate all this from the stage into literature." Thelma, stage struck from an early age, had to a large extent been formed by her exposure to the theater as it still existed in New Orleans in the early years of the twentieth century. She nurtured Ken on this tradition, and he transformed it into his comic masterpiece.

The fact that she could often appear a ridiculous grotesque does not obscure the fact that her strength and perseverance gave her dignity and stature. In the end, her life was not meaningless, as it very nearly was. Without her, there would have been no Ken. Without her stubbornness and her determination, a remarkable novel would never have given its author a kind of immortality and enriched the lives of its many readers. Thelma left a lasting and valuable legacy, and she paid a terrible price for it.

CHAPTER THREE

Publication

Several small coincidences marked for me the appearance of *Confederacy.* In February of 1980, when I read the *Times-Picayne* article announcing that it was to be published, my Italian friend, Roberto, who had last visited me in Louisiana in 1964, was back for another visit. Roberto had been a student of mine in Florence, and later the bookkeeper of our language school. He was with me the last time I saw Ken and the first time I met Thelma.

"Do you remember stopping by to see a friend of mine when I took you to the airport in New Orleans the last time you were here?"

Roberto remembered very well. "Yes, your friend who was writing a book and his strange mother who served us stuffed tomatoes!" Thelma had made an impression.

"Well, my friend is long dead, but his book is about to be published." I showed him the *Times-Picayne* article.

After my first visit with Thelma on Elysian Fields, I returned to Lafayette and placed an order for the soon-to-be published book with a Lafayette bookstore, asking them to telephone me when it came in. Toward the end of April, I was preparing to go to Biloxi, where I had been invited to set up an art exhibition for a meeting of the American Bar Association. The morning I was to leave, the bookstore called to say the shipment of *Confederacy* had arrived. On the way out of town, I swung by the bookstore to get my copy, and that evening I began reading it in the city where Ken had taken his life.

By the time I had finished the first paragraph of the book, I realized that Ken had based the character of Ignatius on Bobby Byrne. The voice, the clothes, the attitude were unmistakable.

Shortly after the book's publication, favorable reviews began to appear. The first one I saw was in *Time.* The critic Paul Gray called the book "terribly funny . . . if a book's price is measured against the laughs it provokes, *A Confederacy of Dunces* is the bargain of the year."

A few days later, I received a phone call from Randy Sue Coburn of the *Washington Star* who wanted to interview me about Ken. Thelma had given her my number. I was quoted in her article as saying "Both parents were definitely eccentric . . . but almost everybody in New Orleans is eccentric. Eccentricity loses its meaning there."

Ms. Coburn told me that she had called Bobby Byrne and asked him if people had told him that he seemed to be the inspiration for the medieval interest of J. Ignatius Reilly. He said that someone had mentioned it to him. "Does that make you want to read the book?" she queried.

"Not desperately . . . I never read best-sellers," he said scornfully.

In early July, I was interviewed by Mary Vespa of *People.*

Ms. Vespa told me that she had also interviewed Bobby Byrne and that he had been very sweet, polite, and gracious to her. He had even given her a copy of Boethius's *Consolation of Philosophy,* the book that shaped Ignatius's "worldview."

When I spoke on the phone to Thelma about the attention the book was getting, she sounded very happy, triumphant even. "You see! You see! That will show those ginks in New York!" Then her voice fell. "But it's all sawdust to me now."

CHAPTER FOUR

Thelma Goes Forth

"I walk in the world for my son."
—A statement repeatedly made by Thelma after the appearance of *Confederacy*.

In the months following the publication of *Confederacy*, Thelma was much in demand at social occasions in New Orleans, and for a time I was her favorite escort. I would drive the two and a half hours across the Atchafalya Swamp to take her to parties where she always dominated the scene, reciting passages from the book and telling with dramatic flair stories from her own life.

One of the first parties Thelma asked me to escort her to was given by one of her former dramatic art students, Miriam Neeb, who lived on North Alexander Street near City Park. When I arrived on a Friday evening in June to pick her up, she was standing just inside her front door, waiting for me, her white-gloved hands clutching her aluminum walker. She was wearing a pink nylon dress and a white pillbox hat that she had decorated with bits of pink and green plastic and pink and green appliquéd felt flowers.

Her white shoes were also embroidered with pink and green flowers. When she moved forward on her walker to greet me, little puffs of talcum powder came from the open toes of her shoes.

As we drove down Elysian Fields, up Burgundy to Esplanade toward City Park, Thelma admired the beautiful homes, and showed me the school on Esplanade where she had studied as a girl. The building had a generally scruffy look. There were half-scrubbed-out graffiti on the façade.

"Look what they've done to it!" Thelma said. "It used to be so well kept. It was a place you could be proud of. I was proud of it. Now look at it!"

The dinner party was held in Miriam's basement garage, which had been converted into a living space with chairs and sofas, lamps on tables, pictures hanging on the paneled walls. There was even a small cooking area with kitchen appliances. The large room still served as a garage, however, and just beyond the fridge was parked a Plymouth Volare. We were greeted by Miriam, a small, dark-haired woman in her late fifties who had impressive bags under her eyes, a cigarette in hand. She was wearing a beige leisure suit. According to Thelma, Miriam had been a star athlete in school.

On entering the room, Thelma exclaimed, "Such spaciousness! I've *never* seen a basement like this!"

Miriam complimented Thelma on her outfit. "Thank you, Miriam. I'm a stickler for everything matching and blending! I remember that someone at St. Joseph's School once said to me, 'Mrs. Toole, when you come in on Monday, we always want to see what you are wearing.' Not that I was a fashion plate, or anything! But they wanted to see what I was wearing! Now, that's cute!"

The other guests were four women about the same age as Miriam, all of whom had been students of Thelma. Only one of them, Yvonne, who was chubby with short gray-blonde hair, had brought her husband. The others were either divorced or widowed.

Leafy, from the Italian family that owned Tujacque's Restaurant in the French Quarter, had very black dyed and over-permed hair. She was wearing a purple pants suit with a light green, flowery blouse, and lots of make-up and jewelry. Her voice was loud and strident.

Dolores was a large woman dressed in black with a single strand of pearls. She hardly spoke all evening.

Nola, dressed in an understated beige suit, was the most elegant of the guests. She was the only one who seemed to have read Ken's book.

A tape recording I made of the party has allowed me to describe the evening with some accuracy. Over a cacophonous babble, Thelma's voice is easily audible, punctuated at times by the squawky voices of Miriam and Leafy.

Miriam had prepared boiled crabs and gumbo and dinner was served unfashionably soon after we arrived. "Mmmm!" said Thelma, "The magnificent effort of all this! Give me a little bit of gumbo, darling. I haven't had gumbo in a long time."

After we had eaten, the evening's entertainment began. Thelma performed. She recited a piece she told us she had written for Ken when he was eleven.

He didn't like sports. I was glad because I didn't want him to be injured and I knew that he had a superior mentality. So I formed a little theatrical troupe, and I had a program at the Marine Hospital on State Street. I wrote this piece for Ken. I read it to him once. He listened. Then I gave him the copy. He studied it one night, and got it down perfectly. I said, "O.K. Son, let me hear it," He did it *perfectly,* slightly better than I did.

The piece was a comic turn called "Various Lovers." In it men of different nationalities sang the praises of their girl friends. Thelma did all the accents. Her audience applauded warmly.

As the evening unfolded, as always, her main topic was Ken.

My son had a tendency to put on weight, but never a flabby fat, and you should have seen the Spartan way he used to eat and used to suffer. When he was going to Tulane, my son used to weigh about 180, and was very sensitive, extremely sensitive . . . oh, sensitive to everything in a Spartan way, and I'd suffer for him.

Thelma also spoke of Ken's early schooling:

He was so superior to all his classmates. They were not ambitious children. I remember that one of them even wanted to be a garbage man! . . . Garbage men have no worries. Just odors.

And Thelma spoke of the book, which was by then already in its seventh printing, and hard to find in New Orleans, where bookstores could not keep it in stock.

I had brought my own copy for her to sign for me that evening, which she did with a flourish: "Appreciation and Warm Regards to Dear Joel from John Kennedy Toole's mother, Thelma Ducoing Toole."

> Look at that book! Look at that picture of Ignatius! You know, before it came out, I told the publisher, "Look, dear, my son was an *artist,* and I am telling you that I will not permit any surrealistic picture of Ignatius, any crackpot, surrealistic hybrid." And he didn't send me a sample, and I was worried. But when he sent me the jacket, long before the book was published, I was delighted! Look at that artist!
>
> When Phillibaum of LSU Press finally told me that he was publishing the book, I made a point of getting acquainted with booksellers. I called about eight booksellers and told them to expect it. I prepared them for it. I didn't bother them. I just told them it was coming—a flash of a second is all I took of their time. And then I got exhausted. I couldn't call anymore. It was *such* an effort!

The tape finished before the party did. I am sure it did not come to such an abrupt end, but I have no taped record and no memories of how the evening concluded.

Miriam gave another dinner party in her garage/salon about nine months later. This time the guest list included only some of Thelma's gentlemen admirers: John Geiser, who had been in school with Ken; David Swoyer, a curator at the New Orleans Museum of Art; Douglas Crawford, a language teacher at Jesuit High School, and me. It was the last time I saw Thelma before the Pulitzer Prizes were announced. There are Polaroid photographs of us sitting around cloth-covered card tables that Miriam had set up, but I did not take any notes on the occasion. Thelma must have brought our hostess a little gift of her favorite talcum powder because a few days after the dinner, I received a letter from Thelma with the following paragraph:

> Sunday afternoon I called Miriam to thank her for the delicious dinner, and the friendly atmosphere which her home generated. Like a "bolt out of the blue," she said: "When Joel told me Mrs. Toole gave me the talcum, I said Mrs. Toole must think I stink!" The vulgarity and "gutterishness" of that being attributed to me! That's the way her relations and friends speak. You were a gentleman not to repeat that to me. I was profoundly shocked! I don't know how clean ignorant women are, but I do know that they eschew perfumes and other sweet scents. My acquaintance with her will continue, but I shall be very circumspect.

One day in September of 1980, Thelma and I had lunch with Sheldon Hackney, then president of Tulane, his wife, and Fred Starr, academic-vice president of Tulane, in the grand mansion on Audubon Place that serves as the president's home. The Hackneys and Dr. Starr were charming and very attentive to Thelma. They were no doubt courting her in hopes of getting Ken's papers for Tulane, but did so with grace, tact, and abundant good will. They brought out the best in Thelma and she performed without the stridency that sometimes crept into her act. A few days later, I had a cordial note from Starr, saying how much he had enjoyed the meeting with "the awesomely vital and engaging Mrs. Toole," and expressing his hopes that eventually Ken's papers would find their way to the Manuscript Division of Tulane's library. Most of them are located there now, including two letters from Ken that he had written to me when I was in California, which I gave to Thelma.

There were other parties, dinners at Sbisa's (a very good restaurant on Decatur Street), and afternoons when I drove Thelma around New Orleans so she could do errands. The air-conditioner in my car was not always dependable. Even when it *was* working, the odor of perfume and powder that Thelma exuded was almost overpowering.

Once, when a friend from France was visiting me, we took Thelma for a picnic in City Park. Afterwards she wrote me: "Champagne, pâté, éclairs, grapes, and a strawberry confection gave me a taste of foods to which I am not accustomed at present. All delectable." In my journal I noted that the menu for the picnic also included Popeye's fried chicken, but Thelma made no mention of this mundane dish in her thank-you note.

One dreary day at the end of November, I drove Thelma to Bart's, a seafood restaurant overlooking Lake Pontchartrain. As we ate seafood platters and watched the yachts of the rich motoring out the channel, Thelma spoke of how hard it had been getting along with so little money. She spoke with contempt of the "club ladies" who used to pay her ten dollars for giving them "a dramatic interpretation of a poem by Poe, plus a complete biographical sketch!" After lunch we went to a convent to see Sister Dorothy, a nun Thelma had known when she taught in

Catholic schools. Sister Dorothy was bent over, feeble, and too tired to spend more than a few minutes with us. Thelma gave her a pink envelope with several ten-dollar bills, which Sister Dorothy gratefully received, and we took our leave. Our last stop on that day was Greenwood Cemetery and the Ducoing family tomb where Ken is buried. A few days later I had a note from her:

> As long as I live, I will send rays of steadfast devotion from my heart to you! Your efficient driving to four different locations, and your impressive appearance, and manner filled me with admiration! Visiting Ken's grave gave me memories that bless and burn. Your kind presence afforded some solace and uplift. Gratefully and lovingly, Thelma

A few weeks later I had another note from her:

> Wednesday, December seventeenth was Ken's birthday. I was so assailed by sadness, loneliness and his loss to the world that I became ill. Today, I have somewhat recovered, and am carrying on my usual duties.

CHAPTER FIVE

Thelma by Thelma

In the spring of 1981 I began to make tape recordings of Thelma talking about her life. Sometimes we made the recordings at her home on Elysian Fields Avenue; other times we would drive to City Park, Audubon Park, or to Lake Pontchartrain and she would talk about whatever she wanted to talk about. When the tape recorder was recording, Thelma was always "on stage," and sometimes seemed a bit less than candid. Some of the most revealing things I learned about her life came when the tape recorder was off. After our sessions I would write down, as quickly as I could, as much of her unrecorded commentary as I could remember.

My reasons for recording Thelma's memories were a little vague. I had some kind of book in mind even then, but also felt that if the book never materialized, the tape recordings in themselves were a good way of preserving her unique history. And Thelma must have had her own ideas.

In July of 1981 the columnist Tommy Griffin wrote in the weekly New Orleans newspaper *Figaro:*

Thelma Toole . . . is presently engaged in a biography

of her life by tape-recording reminiscences with writer Joel Fletcher . . . The tentative title of her book is Thelma Uncurbed . . . I renewed an acquaintance with Mrs. Toole at a Fourth of July party given by Russell Rocke, owner of the Toulouse Theater . . . she was again her gracious, informative self. The above news resulted.

The announcement that we were working on her biography was a bit premature; my description as a "writer" an exaggeration. The title, of course, was Thelma's.

In our first recording session, in her parlor on Elysian Fields, Thelma began at the beginning:

I was born September 3, 1901, in New Orleans on Elysian Fields Avenue, and my earliest recollection of anything is awakening to the fact that I was on a stage. I was in a recital, and I had a costume, but before that, my sister told me, when I was three I participated in my first recital with two five-year olds. They were pulling on their little fairy dresses and I was in the center and I stepped forward. There was a hubbub in the audience. . . . I wanted attention, as young as I was. I wanted them to listen to me, so I blared out, my sister told me. My voice was very powerful and I got a big hand and I don't recall that, but from six years on my costumes thrilled me as I became conscious of them. I always had a leading part, and I also must have had some kind of singing voice.

My first school was St. Peter and St. Paul on St. Claude, just two blocks from my home. I had a good time, but I didn't learn anything from those nuns. They were from Ireland.

Sister Thaddeus was so beautiful. A tall, Irish beauty.

Slightly freckled, very sprightly, and she used to blush a
good deal. Beautiful blue eyes. I was frisky in the classroom . . . high-strung. I behaved, yes, but one time I
had to write twenty times on my big wide tablet: "I am
a bad girl." "Girrrl" Sister Thaddeus used to say. I had
an awful crush on her!

Now in the seventh grade . . . my last year at St. Peter
and St. Paul, the sister . . . she was an elderly woman . . .
faded out . . . very elderly, and her teeth were in bad
condition. I had a crush on her as I never had on the
younger ones. I adored her. She was gentle and kind. I'm
trying to remember her name . . . Sister Julius? Maybe
it was Sister Julius. . . . Well, anyway, I remember the
love I bore for her. I just adored her. I sensed goodness
. . . real religious feeling there . . . you know. It was a
great time, but I didn't learn anything. We were flooded
with prayers . . . prayers in the morning. We'd assemble
out in the hall and sing hymns, and come in and say some
more prayers . . . prayers before lunch and prayers after
lunch, and prayers before leaving at three o'clock.
Fortunately, I already had the ability to read . . . I was a
good reader . . . I was born with that . . . my son was, too.
At St. Peter and St. Paul very little attention was paid to
teaching anything. No attention to geography, no attention to arithmetic. But those were seven happy years.

Probably because of her early experience with ineffectual
nuns, Thelma never took the Catholic Church very seriously.
Her later experiences teaching in Catholic schools left her
even more disenchanted with the Church of Rome.
"Whenever you have to deal with a priest or a nun," she
once told John Geiser, "you always get a headache!"

When I was seventeen I graduated from the high school department of the dramatic art school: The New Orleans College of Oratory and Dramatic Art, and I was given the climactic scene in a play in which the Prince of Wales is leaving this Scotch lass, Jeannie. I was Jeannie, and in the scene I had to tell my mother about my heartbreak, and then the Prince comes to bid me good-bye. It was very good theater. When the play was over, the other actors came out. First the woman who played my mother, and then the prince. The applause was satisfactory. But when I came out, what an ovation! It was so beautiful. When we came home my brother said, "We have an artist in the family." That touched me deeply because he had never been to a recital . . . that was the only one he ever saw and I had been in recitals since I was three. At the graduation exercises I received a gold medal for performance . . . a very beautiful thing, made by Coleman Adler. I went on to the teacher's course of two years and received a certificate for teaching. And that ended my career as a student of dramatic art. I then went into an active career of teaching, for which I was very fitted and was very happy.

I was nineteen when I started teaching at Lakeview Elementary . . . a public school. When I first offered my services to the principal, she said, 'Thelma, can you do that? Do you know how to direct?' I said 'I've never directed a pageant, but I could do it.' And she was surprised when it turned out so beautifully. Every year after that I devised the pageant, designed the costumes, contacted the dressmakers, went to the Canal Street stores to get samples of material. The teachers helped somewhat in meeting the parents and giving them the sketches I made. I taught every dance step. I did the narration for the pageants. I taught the singing. If you act it's hard enough, but directing is much harder. You try getting emotion out of untalented boys and girls! I didn't turn to drink, but I could have! I could have turned to dope! The teachers would teach the lyrics of the songs . . . they cooperated. But I did everything else. I was the dynamic force, and I did it the way I wanted it done!

Then I taught at Holy Angels Academy on St. Claude and directed pageants there. Big outdoor pageants. One was *The Creation of the World* with Lucifer being expelled from Heaven. I think the angel was Michael the Archangel, I don't know . . . but that was the most beautiful thing I've ever done. They used to erect tiers of seats for these pageants, and make a mint, and I never even received a bonus when I directed things like that.

Then I taught dramatics at St. Joseph's High School, Ursuline Academy, for a *very* small salary. But I had four high schools at one time and with the earnings from all four I made a passable living to augment the meager paycheck that John brought home as a car salesman. He was a mathematical wizard and made an enviable record at Warren Easton High School. He was a champion debater. He was brilliant. But by some quirk of mind he chose to be an automobile salesman . . . no standing in the community, no decent income, causing great distress in our forty-five years of marriage. And for all those years, I was the main breadwinner. Not that I didn't love teaching and putting on pageants. I expressed myself! It was art! It was something over which I had control! It was something I had a knowledge of!

When I married we moved into a brand new, very

beautiful double on Orleans, opposite City Park. It was tastefully furnished and delighted us and we had company about twice a week, and over the weekend it was constant partying with our own very witty group. I remember one time, one man . . . I can't remember his name . . . extremely funny . . . said something that sent me into guffaws. I beckoned to him and I put him in the kitchen and I closed the door and he couldn't return because I was in paroxysms of laughter, and I was suffering and he stayed in that kitchen. He'd knock on the door and I wouldn't permit him to come back in the living room . . . that's the kind of effervescent company we had!

And then I started to teach in the home. I couldn't teach any more at Lakeview or in any of the public schools because the Orleans Parish School Board had an ordinance then against hiring married women as teachers. So I taught at home: speech and dramatic art and word usage. It was a nice little source of income . . . very relaxed, and something I had never done. I taught adults. They were very receptive and it was a very happy time. And then later I was approached by some nuns to teach in the Catholic high schools, and I thought it over for a year and then accepted it. For a very meager salary I produced impressive theatrical productions. It was part of my life, and with sixteen years of dramatic art training I was very good at it. It really gave me a wonderful outlook. I had a long teaching career. I was very successful. Particularly my five years at the Convent of the Good Shepherd for Delinquent Girls. I told Mother Superior that I didn't want to hear about their backgrounds. I just wanted to teach them and accept them from that point on. Now, I gave those girls favorable attention, and there was a Ladies' Guild that sewed . . . wealthy women, women of leisure . . . and they provided any costume I designed. Those were the most substantial years of my teaching. I used to approach presidents of Canal Street stores to ask them for merchandise for the girls: Godchaux's, D. H. Holmes, Maison Blanche, La Biche . . . I also provided them with perfume from a local drugstore and provided corsages for them from a florist when we had a program for their mothers. Those were fine, toweringly successful programs. I received letters from the girls when they left . . . very heartwarming to know what I did for them.

Thelma could also be very funny about her experiences with the New Orleans Catholic schools.

She often mentioned that she was going to write a paper about the "pa-roach-al" schools of New Orleans. She would recite bits of it in an *almost* Irish Channel accent (though she was not able to bring herself to abandon completely her elocutionary principles and turn all her *ths* into *ds!*)

I'm going to write about dem sweet Sisters! I can tell you! I can tell you dem sweet Sisters am Saints. Why, dem sweet Sisters made a vow not to have no money, and the only money they got was the nickels and dimes that we brought them. And once a year we had to give to the Pope and Sister said: "I don't want no nickels and dimes and quarters," she said. "I want dollar bills." Well, my mother didn't have a dollar extra so I brought my quarter. The first time I ever see Sister get mad!

And dem sweet Sisters didn't travel. They only went

to places outside New Orleans. I think they went to Franklin. They went to places they called "Mother Houses." They didn't travel, so we didn't have any geography. They didn't know there was something called "geography."

And dem sweet Sisters took a vow of obedience, and we was all obedient, too. We listened to our mommas and we listened to our Sisters. Our mommas said, "Never talk back to the Sisters, or they'll faint."

Listening to Thelma do her set pieces, one realized where Ken got his gift for mimicry and for creating characters with authentic New Orleans flavor. She provided the ore that he refined and made into literature.

Thelma spoke of her ancestry, a mix of Irish and French Creole. One of her Creole ancestors, Jean Baptiste Ducoing, had fought in the Battle of New Orleans, and is buried in St. Louis Cemetery Number One. When Ken was growing up, she sometimes took him to see his ancestor's tomb. Many of her other antecedents were working-class Irish who came to the United States in the great waves of immigration in the nineteenth century. Her father, Paul Ducoing, was something of a dandy, and an opera and theater buff. Ducoing served for thirty years as probate clerk of the Civil District Court, and had many important political connections. Though far from being rich, he moved in wealthy circles. When Thelma married, she said her in-laws, impressed by her father's style and connections, thought John was marrying money, but, of course, she hadn't any. Thelma adored her father, and early on realized he was not perfect.

"When I was about nine, I discovered that my father had

a mistress," she told me once when the tape recorder was not running. "I found out that he took her on a trip to Cuba, and I wondered why he had not taken my mother."

> My father, who was a very natty dresser, often dined with society judges and other important types. We didn't see much of him. But when he did eat with us, at the dinner table, he didn't chat with my mother, he didn't ask us children how we were progressing in school. He wasn't interested in such matters. He was a *bon vivant,* a man of the world. He told us about the theater and the opera. He was not concerned with domestic life. He is the one who instilled in me my love of the theater.

Thelma and her sisters often attended the theater when they were growing up. Like Thelma herself, one of her father's sisters was stage-struck, and she would take her nieces to see plays at the Dauphine, the Orpheum, and the Tulane theaters.

When Thelma was young, there was much theater to be seen in New Orleans. It was a city with an important theatrical history. In 1938, the year after Ken was born, the Federal Writers' Project of the Works Progress Administration published the excellent *New Orleans City Guide.* The chapter on theater in New Orleans traces its origin to the arrival in 1791 of a "homeless refugee band of actors and actresses who had fled the terrors of a murderous Negro uprising in the French West Indies." This troupe, led by a Monsieur Louis Tabary, is the first recorded mention of theater in a city where theater soon was thriving. The *Guide* attributes its success to the "pleasure-loving Latins," who made up the majority of the population of the city. By the time of the Civil War, New Orleans was second only to New York City in the number of theaters and the quality of professional performances. In the nineteenth century many world-famous actors appeared in New Orleans, the most important stop on a southern tour. Edwin Booth, James Brutus Booth, Jenny Lind, Sarah Bernhardt, Joe Jefferson (who was a part-time resident of Louisiana) were a few of the then famous stars to appear on New Orleans stages. When Thelma was born in New Orleans in 1901, a strong theatrical tradition still existed in New Orleans, and it continued up until the Great Depression. In the early years of the twentieth century, there was much for the theater-obsessed to feast on in New Orleans. The *City Guide* lists Julia Marlow, George Arliss, Richard Mansfield, Maude Adams, De Wolf Hopper, Robert Mantell, Katherine Cornell, and Anna Held as among those appearing at the Tulane Theater on Baronne Street in the first three decades of the century. Their names are not familiar today, but they were the stars of their time.

> At the old Dauphine . . . it's been torn down now . . . there was a path leading to the actor's entrance, and my sisters and my aunt used to hang around there waiting for the actors. That's something that I have never done . . . hang around waiting for actors! And my aunt had a very classy voice and she would talk to the actors when they came out. I never did. But we were all crazy about the theater, crazy! We saw everybody who came to New Orleans . . . many of the best actors and actresses. Once I saw Ethel Barrymore at the Tulane, and she came out

on the stage so drunk she could hardly walk, much less act!

The New Orleans theatrical scene was a major influence on Thelma when she was young. It played a more important role in educating and forming her than did the Catholic Church; the theater had more importance in her eyes than the Church, which she knew principally through the poorly-educated nuns whom she was fond of but largely unimpressed by. Theater became her religion.

The Great Depression curtailed much of the theatrical richness of New Orleans, and, as S. Frederick Starr has pointed out, by the time Ken was growing up, the nineteenth century histrionic theatrical tradition with which Thelma totally identified "lived on only in her parlor."

The family home at 1020 Elysian Fields Avenue must have been rather grand, built when the Faubourg Marigny was an exclusive suburb for the Creole aristocracy of New Orleans. By the turn of the last century, when Thelma was born there, most of the wealthier Creole families had moved elsewhere, and the Marigny was becoming a neighborhood of poor Sicilian immigrants. It was, of course, the neighborhood, the very street, where Tennessee Williams set *A Streetcar Named Desire.*

In an unguarded moment, Thelma told me that when she was a young girl one of her father's bachelor brothers had committed suicide. "What shame it brought on the family," she said, but would say no more about it.

Thelma had three brothers: Paul Apollonius, Arthur, and George. She had a sister, Anna, and a step-sister from her mother's first marriage, Margaret Ann Garvey, who was also known as "Dolly." Thelma was particularly attached to her sister, Anna, who was nine years older.

She was a great girl, a schoolteacher, interested in the theater. She looked very French. (I looked very Irish.) A beautiful girl, and very skillful. She was always making hats and framing pictures, and we were always going to dressmakers. At that time everybody was buying yard goods and having dresses made. We used to buy patterns, or else make a sketch for the dressmaker to follow. Anna bought a sewing machine after she married, realizing she would have turned into a wonderful dressmaker. She taught in grade school. She didn't graduate in dramatic art like I did. I fussed at her for that. She studied dramatic art for eight or ten years . . . I had sixteen. She had my voice . . . theatrical contralto, and she loved her family. She loved her father. He loved her. Father's have crushes on their daughters and sons have a romantic feeling for their mothers. Usually that's the way it goes. To be honest and candid, Anna was the star of the family. She was our father's favorite. He took her to New York when she finished the eighth grade. He never even took me across the river!

Anna married Oliver Hingle from a nice family over on Governor Nicholls. He was handsome and lovable and generous. He tried to kiss me once after they had married and I pushed him away! But they adored each other and they weren't married for very long when Anna got sick and died. They were only married for ten months. He never got over it. He remarried three years later, but he didn't love his second wife. He stayed in touch with the family and we know he never got over her. And then one day he threw himself off a Canal Street building. I think it was Maison Blanche. He jumped off and crashed through a glass roof, and killed himself. A friend of mine was there when it happened.

Ken's was not the first family suicide to which Thelma had been a witness. First her uncle, then her former brother-in-law.

Thelma did not say anything about her youngest brother, George, but in the Toole archive at Tulane there is a letter, dated July, 1962, from Ken in Puerto Rico to his parents. In it he writes that he had recently seen the movie *Light in the Piazza,* which deals with a love affair between two retarded young people. (Bobby Byrne after seeing the movie had remarked to me that "they should have called it *Dim Light in the Piazza!*")

Ken wrote:

> So much of the movie was a cinematic revelation of a case which we've known so well for the past twenty-four years this June, and I experienced a 'shock of recognition' so many times during the course of the story's unwinding.

Ken's allusion is partially explained by another letter in the archive from his uncle Arthur asking a friend, the city coroner, to help him place his brother George in the Psychiatric Department of Charity Hospital. George had grown too difficult to manage at home.

Thelma mentioned, but did not dwell upon, the two

suicides that had affected her when she was young, and she never spoke to me at all of the mental problems of her brother George. I first learned that there had been something wrong with him when I came across the two letters in the Tulane archive which speak of his problem but do not elaborate. Suicide and mental illness in the family were not topics she wished to discuss.

The happy early years of her marriage did not last. Before Ken was born, John was fired from his job selling cars for the Stevens Motor Company, and they lost the house on Orleans Street and all their furniture. They had to go back to live with John's parents. John eventually found a job as a mechanic at a smaller salary than he had been earning as a salesman.

> He was too proud to accept the tips as other mechanics did. One day the Brach candy heir arrived in a flashy car with a beautiful blonde. John was so taken by the beauty of the blonde that he refused to accept a twenty-dollar tip that Brach offered to the several mechanics who worked on the car. Brach said "Okay. I'll send you a basket with twenty dollars of our finest candies!" The basket never came. John would give driving lessons and do all kinds of errands for his customers, and they took advantage of him. He even borrowed $300 so Judge Rudy Becker could make a down payment on a car . . . and then I had to go to see the Judge and try to collect from him! When Ken was born, John gave a fifty-dollar tip to the wealthy doctor who delivered him. I didn't even get a bottle of perfume!

By the time Ken was born in 1937, Thelma had realized

that she was going to be the chief breadwinner of the family. She more or less gave up on her husband, and concentrated all her energies on earning a living and nurturing her son, who became the real focus of her life. She insulated Ken from what she felt would be negative influences. She did not encourage him to spend time with his Toole cousins because she thought they were too ordinary and not worthy company for him. She chose the children he was allowed to associate with, and it is not surprising that he grew up with few childhood friends.

> I never invited neighborhood ladies over to drink coffee or went to drink coffee and gossip with the neighbors. Instead, I lavished all my free time on my son. When he was very small, every day I could, I would take him for a long walk in City Park, and we would see the children of the wealthy with their nurses. I was the only mother there with her own child! That is why we were so close. When he was grown up, we would sit around the kitchen table and make up "low class" dialogues to amuse ourselves while we sipped a highball. That's the way we used to relax.

Ken had a very protected childhood, but as he entered his teenage years, economic necessity forced him to leave the cultural cocoon his mother had woven and find work in the outside world. To help with his parents' almost always desperate need for money, he worked shelving books at the Latter Memorial Library on St. Charles Avenue, worked in the stockroom of McCrory's five and dime on Canal Street, typed menus for Wise's Cafeteria. At least two of his jobs must have supplied material for *Confederacy:* Ken worked as a hot dog vendor, not on Bourbon Street like Ignatius, but at Tulane football games. And he worked as a clerk in the Haspel Brothers clothing factory, which his creative imagination transformed into the Levy Pants Factory.

As Ken grew up, Thelma felt certain that he would live up to the high expectations she had for him, compensating for her profound disappointment in her husband. When Ken graduated from Fortier High School, he was given the award for "Most Intelligent Student." He then won a National Merit Scholarship to Tulane. At first, encouraged by his father, he enrolled in the School of Engineering, but he didn't like it. He soon became an English major and made excellent grades for the rest of his undergraduate career. In his senior year he was voted into Phi Beta Kappa and won a Woodrow Wilson Fellowship. He went to Columbia University for his master's degree, writing his master's thesis on the obscure sixteenth-century English author John Lyly, whose very obscurity must have appealed to Ken's enjoyment of the absurd. He then enrolled as a part-time Ph.D. candidate at Columbia and taught a few courses at Hunter College. In 1959 he accepted an appointment as instructor at the University of Southwestern Louisiana, where I met him in the summer of 1960. The next year he was drafted and sent to boot camp. Repeating the triumphs he had experienced in grammar school, high school, college, and graduate school, the army was a very positive experience for Ken. Much like Proust, he was an unlikely and unexpected success as a soldier. He was both amused and pleased when he was named "Soldier of the Month" at Fort Buchanan in Puerto Rico.

Nick Polites saw Ken in New Orleans over the Christmas holidays in 1962. Hearing that they had met, I wrote: "What changes have sun and rum wrought in Ken?"

Nick replied: "The sun seems to be winning. Ken looked healthy and tanned, but perhaps beneath the bronze surface he is dissipated. I really don't know, except that perhaps he may be impervious to alcohol. . . . The army is spoiling him, as all people and institutions spoil him by flattery."

When Ken was released from the army, he made what must have been the worst decision of his life, though perhaps he thought he had little choice in the matter. Instead of returning to New York and his work at Columbia and Hunter, yielding to pressure from his parents, he found the teaching job in New Orleans. He planned to continue to work on his novel about which he had already received much encouragement from Simon and Schuster, and he probably genuinely believed that he could be more productive working on the book by staying in New Orleans. After he returned there from Puerto Rico, he wrote me: "Although you may not agree, life here is certainly better than the masochism of living in New York, which has become the Inferno of America, the American Dream as Apocalypse. And I'd never be able to try to write anything if I were caught up in the Columbia-Hunter axis."

Ken moved back in with Thelma and John at what was a particularly difficult time in their lives. John was retired and had become almost totally deaf. Thelma was having great difficulty finding work. Times had changed. School pageants were out of fashion and elocution lessons no longer in demand. There was very little money coming in.

A letter in the Tulane archive from Ken to his parents, written while he was still in the army in Puerto Rico, tells them that he is trying to arrange for them to receive more money from an allotment paid by the army. There is no indication whether or not he was successful in doing so.

After Ken took the job at Dominican College, he supplanted Thelma as the breadwinner of the family, and came to be more and more under her thumb. Several of his friends told him he was making a mistake. J.C. Broussard, Bobby Byrne, Nick Polites, and perhaps others, foresaw the terrible situation he was getting into and advised him to leave New Orleans. But he didn't, or perhaps he felt he couldn't. He had pinned his hopes to the success of *Confederacy* and when it became apparent that Simon and Schuster were not going to publish it, instead of trying to send it elsewhere, he seems to have given up. He stopped writing and enrolled as a part-time graduate student at Tulane, working toward a Ph.D. But his heart must not have been in it. He had been so groomed for success by Thelma that he could not deal with this setback in his life. He must have begun to feel that he would be a failure like his father. Thelma, in her pain and anger, must have lashed out at him, as I had seen her, when she was in a foul mood, lash out at me and others for no good reason.

In the interview Bobby Byrne gave to Carmine Palumbo, he related something that had happened when Ken, after his return home, was visiting Bobby in New Orleans. Bobby told Ken the story of how his Aunt May used to get annoyed with Thelma because she was always talking about her genius son. Bobby said that Ken had seemed very surprised to hear this. "My mother spends all her time telling me how stupid I am," Ken said. After his death, Thelma had only the highest praise for Ken, then always her genius son, but it was probably a different story when he was alive and they were living in close quarters, and age and poverty and disappointment were closing in on her. Patricia Rickels believes that an argument with Thelma must have triggered Ken's final breakdown that led to his fleeing New Orleans and ultimately to his suicide. Patricia and Milton Rickels were among Ken's closest friends in Lafayette. They were both on the English faculty at Southwestern, and Ken spent much of his free time with them and their young son, to whom he gave many of his own childhood books. During the period after Ken disappeared, Thelma was convinced that Ken was staying with the Rickels and telephoned them constantly begging them to let her speak to him. Finally, she told Pat: "I know that he does not want to speak to me, but just tell me that he is there and that he is all right." Pat realized that Ken and Thelma must have had some kind of quarrel. "After they found Ken's body, Thelma would never speak to me again," Pat told me. "I think it was because she realized I knew too much about why he had disappeared."

"I have no time for people who fall by the wayside!" I heard Thelma exclaim on more than one occasion. Had Thelma made Ken feel that he had fallen by the wayside, reinforcing his own feelings of defeat and futility? The myth that Thelma propagated after Ken's suicide was that he killed himself out of despair at Gottlieb's rejection, but that could not have been the immediate cause. The apparent

failure of his novel certainly must have contributed to the
hopelessness that had begun to weigh on Ken so heavily,
but three years had elapsed between his final communica-
tion with Gottlieb and his death in Biloxi. At the end of
their correspondence, Gottlieb, who had given him much
encouragement, left a door open for him. Ken chose not to
use it.

Thelma preferred to talk about the earlier part of her life,
before Ken's suicide changed her world so drastically, but
she also spoke of the dark period after it occurred.

After she learned of Ken's suicide ninety miles away
from New Orleans in Biloxi, Thelma arranged to have his
body shipped to the Schoen Funeral Home on Elysian
Fields Avenue, just a few blocks down the street from her
childhood home. She did not tell anyone about the service
held at the nearby St. Peter and St. Paul Church. There
were only three people at Ken's funeral: Thelma and John
Toole and Beulah Matthews, the black nurse who had
sometimes looked after Ken when he was a child. The
States/Item ran a brief obituary. Dominican, where Ken had
been teaching, gave a memorial service for Ken, even
though it was a Catholic school and he had been a suicide.

Thelma stopped teaching, stopped playing her piano,
and withdrew from the world. "I became a robot woman,"
she said. She stayed at home and nursed her husband as he
declined into illness and senility, and brooded on the death
of her son.

For two years Ken's manuscript sat on top of an armoire
in what had been his room. When Thelma finally focused
on it and decided she would try to get it published, she

found a mission that would again give meaning to her life. Her first reaction to the bulky manuscript after Ken's death was that she did not want it published because she was afraid it would remind people of Ken's disgraceful death which had brought shame to the Toole and Ducoing families. Only gradually did she change her mind and come to feel that it had to be published as a validation of her son's genius.

She began sending the manuscript out to possible publishers. She sent it out ten times and each time it came back with a rejection slip. "Each time it came back I died a little," she said.

But even further bad fortune could not deflect nor extinguish her newly found purpose in life. When her husband died two years later, there was less than $300 in their savings account. A few months later she tripped over a trunk in the bathroom and broke her arm. She lay in the dark for twenty-four hours until her brother, Arthur, found her. After stays in a series of hospitals, unable to care for herself, she went to live in a nursing home. It was more than she could bear. Swallowing her pride, she telephoned Arthur, with whom she had long had a difficult relationship, and asked him to come get her. There was nowhere else for her to go but the small cottage Arthur had built in 1960 near the site of their former childhood home on Elysian Fields Avenue.

Thelma's life seemed to have come full circle, a grim and hopeless circle. She was seventy-five years old and in poor health. She had little money and was completely dependent on a brother who, she believed, had cheated her out of part of her inheritance. She was about to give up on the book. The form rejection letters hurt too much and she had run out of places to send it. But life had not quite defeated her. One day she read in the *Times-Picayune* that Walker Percy was in town teaching a course at Loyola University. She put on her best dress, trimmed in lace, a nice pair of shoes, a white hat, and a pair of white gloves. She put the worn, smudged, and somewhat tattered manuscript in her purse, and made Arthur drive her uptown to Loyola, resolved that she was going to see Mr. Percy and demand that he read her son's masterpiece.

ft, below: the log cabin that served as Bobby Byrne's study, and where he played his harpsichord. Above: the room tached to Ralph Lynch's garage, where Bobby lived when he knew Ken in Lafayette. (Collection of the author)

ight, the courtyard of the Napoleon House where the author spent an evening with Ken and Bobby Byrne, tening to them gossip about their uptown neighborhood. (Photo by Jackie Brenner)

'L English faculty, 1960. From left, Ken is the last one in the top row. Bobby Byrne, the inspiration for iatius Reilly, is the third one in the top row. Between Byrne and Ken is Jack Ward, whose wife, Ann, 1 found very attractive. Ken's other friends at USL are standing together in the front row. Beginning with rth from left: J.C. Broussard, Milton Rickels, Muriel Price, Patricia Rickels, and Nicholas Polites. ourtesy Dupré Library, University of Louisiana at Lafayette)

Left, Elisabeth Montgomery, Ken's landlady in Lafayette, dressed as the Empress of Japan for a Lafay[ette] Mardi Gras Ball. (Collection of the author)

Right, 390 Audubon Street, where Ken and his parents were living the last time the author saw him a[?] (Photo by Jackie Brenner)

The apartment building on Convent Street where Ken lived in Lafayette, behind the home of his landl[ady] Elisabeth Montgomery. (Collection of the author)

Ken on the beach in Biloxi. He often enjoyed excursions to this Gulf Coast town during undergraduate days. In his last letter to the author, Ken wrote: "The Gulf Coast looks better when you're not there." He committed suicide in Biloxi in March of 1969. (Courtesy Tulane Special Collections)

Sazerac Bar of the Roosevelt Hotel (now the Fairmont), where Ken, J. C. Broussard, and Nicholas ites spent an afternoon together. Each went home and wrote the author a letter describing the event. (Photo ackie Brenner)

Left, Studio portrait of Thelma, New Orleans, circa 1925. The photograph of his mother which Ken h[...] with him while in the army in Puerto Rico. (Collection of the author)

Right, A pencil drawing by Ken, probably of Thelma. (Courtesy Tulane Special Collections)

7632 Hampson Street, the house in which the Tooles were living when Ken committed suicide. (Phot[...] Jackie Brenner)

Two photographs of Thelma as a child " . . . my earliest recollection of anything is awakening to the fact that I was on a stage. I was in a recital, and I had a costume . . . " (Courtesy Tulane Special Collections)

Arthur Ducoing, Thelma's brother, with whom she had a difficult relationship and with whom she lived on Elysian Fields Avenue at the end of her life. (Courtesy Tulane Special Collections)

P. A. Ducoing, Thelma's father, "something of dandy, and an opera and theater buff." He served thirty years as probate clerk of the Civil District Cou (Courtesy Tulane Special Collections)

Anna, Thelma's sister, and Oliver Hingle, her husband. They were married for only ten months before Anna died of influenza. He later committed suicide by throwing himself off a building on Canal Street. (Courtesy Tulane Special Collections)

...nale of a spring recital, Ken as narrator, at ...e Lakeview School of Speech and Dramatic ...rt. Thelma directed the recital. (Courtesy ...lane Special Collections)

John Toole, Ken's father, *"a mathematical wizard . . . a champion debater."* He never lived up to Thelma's expectations, and she became the main breadwinner of the family. (Courtesy Tulane Special Collections)

Ken as a child, in costume. (Courtesy Tulane Special Collections)

Ken was about sixteen when this photograph was taken, the age at which he wrote The Neon Bible. *(Collection of the author)*

n as a soldier, at which he was a surprising ccess. (Courtesy Tulane Special Collections)

Thelma playing and singing at her baby grand a few weeks after the publication of Confederacy. (Collection of the author)

The second dinner party in Miriam Neeb's garage/salon. From left: Thelma, John Geiser (partially obscured), David Swoyer, Douglas Crawford, Miriam Neeb.(Collection of the author)

Publicity card for the Grove Press edition of Confederacy *of* Confederacy *sent to the author by Thelma is May of 1981. (Collection of the author)*

Thelma arriving at Rockefeller Center for the taping of the Tom Snyder Show, April 1981. (Collection of the author)

Left, Barney Rosset, head of Grove Press, and Thelma at the Warwick Hotel reception hosted by Grove. *woman in the background is Barbara Clare, an antiques dealer and friend of the author and Thel (Collection of the author)

Right, Thelma signing books at the Warwick Hotel reception. The man with the bow tie on the righ Nicholas Polites, friend of both Ken and the author. (Collection of the author)

Thelma and Anthony Quinn in the Green room before the taping of the Tom Snyder Show. (Collectio the author)

Left, Thelma in New Orleans, June 1981. (Photo by Philip Gould)

Right, Thelma performing at the Warwick Hotel reception. (Collection of the author)

picnic in City Park. From left: Jean Nicolas (a visitor from France), Douglas Crawford, Thelma ...laiming. (Collection of the author)

Left, Doonie Guibet, Ken's best friend from childhood, being arrested for murder. (Collection the author)

Right, Kenneth Holditch, to whom Thelma left her interest in The Neon Bible, *next to the statue of Igna J. Reilly in front of the former D. H. Holmes department store on Canal Street. (Collection of the autho*

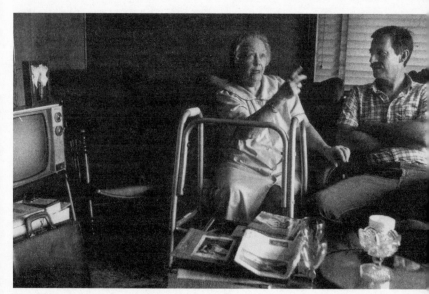

Thelma "on stage" in the living room of 1016 Elysian Fields Avenue with the author. (Photo by Philip Gou

Left, A Lucky Dog, the inspiration for Paradise Vendors in Confederacy. *(Photo by Jackie Brenner)*

Right, Constantinople Street, near the river, where Ignatius lived with his momma, Irene. (Photo by Jackie Brenner)

Schwegmann's Super Market, across the street from the house Thelma shared with her brother Arthur on Elysian Fields Avenue. (Collection of the author)

Ken and Thelma's tomb in the Greenwood Cemetery. (Photo by Jackie Brenner)

Schoen Funeral Home on Elysian Fields Avenue, which handled the arrangements for the funerals of Ken and Thelma. (Collection of the author)

CHAPTER SIX

John Toole

In the story of Ken and Thelma, Thelma's husband, John, is a peripheral figure: the bright young man of promise who never lived up to expectations, led a feckless, marginal life, and was never able to provide a proper living for his family. He became the object of Thelma's scorn.

Like Ignatius in *Confederacy,* John Toole never had a job worthy of his education and was a gifted underachiever. But how did Ken feel about his father? A single letter in the Toole archive at Tulane tells a great deal about Ken and John's relationship.

In 1962, while Ken was in the army in Puerto Rico, John developed shingles, and Ken wrote a letter to him expressing his great distress over his father's illness:

> I love you very much, Dad, and I hope and pray that this painful infection passes. You have always been so good, so kind to me that it hurts me to know that you are in pain. All my love, Ken

I was struck by this unexpectedly tender expression of love for a father by his son, which seems to indicate that while Thelma may have been the most influential person in Ken's life, his father was also a person of consequence in his eyes. He obviously felt a great affection for his father, and seems not to have shared his mother's contempt, though he must have been aware of it. In Ken's last years, as he became more and more convinced of his own failure, he must have identified with his father and the unimpressive role he played in the eyes of Thelma and the world.

When Ken went to Tulane, he first studied engineering because his father wanted him to do so, though it took only a few weeks for him to realize that he was, indeed, his mother's son, and the seeds that she had planted in him had firmly taken root. "I'm losing my culture," he told her, and switched his major to English. Thelma had won the battle for her son's soul, though it had hardly been a fight.

CHAPTER SEVEN
Travels with Thelma

In early spring of 1981, Grove Press planned to publish the mass-market paperback edition of *Confederacy.* Lee Wiggins, director of promotion and publicity for Grove, wrote Thelma in February about the possibility of her appearing on various talk shows. She had first in mind the Phil Donahue show, but also mentioned "David Susskind, Dick Cavitt, Tom Snider [sic], 20/20 and PM Magazine."

In early March, Thelma wrote me:

> For the past two months, I have been under inordinate pressure, which has impaired my already poor health . . . It is important that I try to regain some semblance of composure and stamina, because of the prospective talk show which Grove Press is trying to plan. If that event ever materializes, the delight of your escort service will be deeply appreciated.

I must not have replied to the letter because a few days later she wrote:

> Diana Durham [a friend of Thelma's, probably one of

her former students] is a good, generous friend, and her espousing "Confederacy" makes me feel so tender to her. However, announcing that she wanted to travel with me to Chicago (if it ever materializes) startled me. If I do go, I will need utter concentration, because preparing, enplaning and deplaning would exhaust me completely. Meeting Phil Donahue, I would be assured and composed for the reason that I "walk in the world" for my son. I feel I am a humble, but worthy representative of him.

Diana doesn't realize the daily loneliness and suffering I endure.

Dearest, you didn't reveal your reaction to the aforesaid matter.

The trip to Chicago and the Phil Donahue show never materialized, but the day after Thelma wrote me the above, she received a letter from Florence Jumonville, chairman of the Louisiana Library Association, informing her that *Confederacy* had been given the 1980 Louisiana Literary Award for fiction and inviting her to the presentation ceremony in Shreveport. Thelma was delighted and asked me to accompany her. At that moment, Thelma had nothing but praise for Ms. Jumonville and the Louisiana Library Association, but after the fiasco of the trip to Shreveport, they were entered on her list of villains, from which they were never removed. The LLA meeting fell behind schedule as the keynote speaker droned on and on telling one inane joke after another. "To think they would have invited someone of *his* caliber to address a meeting like this! It makes you wonder about librarians in general, doesn't it?" she whispered to me. As the speaker went on far beyond his allotted time, we realized that in order to catch our flight back to New Orleans, we would have to leave before Thelma made her acceptance remarks, which she had labored over. She was in a fury all the way back to New Orleans.

A week later I was in Atlanta. I noted in my journal:

> A light was flashing on the phone when I got back to my room last night. Messages to call Thelma as Ken's novel had just been awarded the Pulitzer Prize. When I got her she sounded happy, tired, but calm. Three TV crews had been at the house that afternoon and she said she was so excited that only ten minutes after the interview began did she remember to finish buttoning her house dress.

When I called her the next day, a reporter answered the phone and said that Thelma couldn't speak right then because she was being interviewed by the *New York Times.* When I finally did get her on the phone, she told me, "Honey, people are calling to congratulate me who don't even know how to *spell* Pulitzer!" The next morning the story about Ken and the Pulitzer was on the front page of the *New York Times,* and Thelma appeared on the CBS morning news, which I did not get to see.

A few days later when I was back in Lafayette, Thelma called to tell me that Grove Press, who were, of course, more than delighted that the book they were about to bring out had won a Pulitzer, had arranged for her to appear on the Tom Snyder show. She asked if I could make the trip to New York with her. I was not immediately sure that I would be able to go, and Thelma exploded at me. I had seen evidence of her unforgiving temper before, but this was the first time it had been directed at me, and I was taken aback. As it turned out, I was able to escort her, and when I gave her this news all was forgiven and, it seemed by her, forgotten.

Grove Press booked us on an early morning Eastern Airlines flight from New Orleans to LaGuardia on April 21, and by noon we were in our rooms at the luxurious Berkshire Place Hotel. While waiting for Lee Wiggins of Grove, we let room service bring us an elegant lunch of steamed salmon and *nouvelle cuisine* vegetables. Thelma was overcome. "I've never been used to luxury!" she said. "Sure, I've seen luxury; I know what luxury looks like. But I don't want luxury!"

This trip to New York was to be very unlike the visit she made when Ken was teaching at Hunter and studying at Columbia. Then she had stayed at the Taft Hotel, once very grand, but then well past its prime, and walked the twenty-five blocks to his apartment each day. "Don't spend your money taking me to the movies, honey," she told me she had said to Ken, who was struggling to get by in New York on his meager salary from Hunter. Thelma had suggested a cheaper form of entertainment: "Let's watch newsreels. I like newsreels." On this trip to New York, Thelma was staying in a very posh hotel, and she herself was the news.

Lee arrived, a tall, attractive, dark-haired woman in her early thirties, and asked us to be in the lobby at a certain time that afternoon to await the limousine that would take us to the NBC studio for the taping of the show. By Thelma's order we were in the lobby fifteen minutes early. She was wearing a handsome, navy blue suit with white gloves, white shoes, and her white hat made of artificial flowers. The hat had been spruced up for the occasion by a generous application of talcum powder that concealed the gray of age. I made a Polaroid of Thelma getting out of the limo at Rockefeller Center. Her right hand is gripping an armrest for support, and her left hand is raised in a regal wave. I told her she looked just like the Queen Mother of England.

In the green room we found Anthony Quinn, who was to precede Thelma on the *Tomorrow Show.* Thelma, far from being intimidated by his fame, treated him as an equal and told him about her genius son. A photograph I took of them shows Thelma leaning forward toward a rather alarmed looking Quinn. In introducing me, she said, "Mr. Quinn, I am sure that you have an appreciation of the finer things, including art. I would like to introduce you to my escort, Mr. Fletcher, who deals in the finer things. I think you might be very interested in seeing some of the beautiful and extremely rare works he deals in. You must tell him how he can get in touch with you!" I gave Mr. Quinn an embarrassed smile, but to my amazement he obeyed. He picked up a pad of yellow, lined paper, wrote "Anthony Quinn / Adams Hotel / #2 E. 86th Street / New York City," ripped it out, and handed it to me. He must have been very relieved when he was summoned to the cameras.

Before Thelma's turn on TV, a production assistant came in to give her a few tips. "I don't know if you've ever had any experience in front of a camera," she told Thelma, "but don't be afraid to make a few gestures with your hands while you are talking so you won't seem so stiff." The poor girl had no idea to whom she was giving advice. Thelma's eyebrows went up and she flipped her wrist in a dramatic flourish that must have taken the girl's breath away. "I guess you have done this sort of thing before," she said, and quickly disappeared.

Thelma was called into the studio and I watched her performance on a monitor. Tom Snyder, with ponderous earnestness, began: "Next up, a woman of rare perseverance, who for years has been fighting for recognition for a book written by her son eleven years ago. Last week, that book, which his mother finally had published, won the Pulitzer Prize for fiction. Mrs. Thelma Moore is a woman who never gave up her fight for her son's literary recognition."

By the end of the introduction, Snyder had been cued that Thelma's name was Toole, and corrected himself, though later in the interview he did refer to her as Mrs. O'Toole. Thelma was unfazed. She saw the studio audience and, ignoring the camera and Snyder, addressed it. When he asked her why she had not put her son's book "back in the drawer and forgot about it," she stared at the faces in front of her and began her story:

> Because I knew, from his birth, there was an aura of greatness. He was a magnificent baby, and he had the appearance of a six-month old child, and he was the talk of the nursery department in Touro Infirmary. They told me he was the only baby they had ever seen who had facial expressions. The nurses would crowd around the crib and admire him. Well, he lived up to that promise, and when he was three years old, I took him to a nursery school, and when he was four, he went to a public school kindergarten, and the teacher thought he was a little prince!

Snyder was unnerved by Thelma's talking to the audience instead of to him. "Why aren't you looking at me?" he demanded.

Thelma realized her mistake. "Indeed!" she said. "It's dedicated to you! Pardon my being so remiss!"

Thelma told the story of how Ken wrote the book while he was in the army in Puerto Rico, and mentioned that the title had come from a quotation by Jonathan Swift: "When a true genius appears in the world, you may know him by this sign, that the dunces are all in confederacy against him."

"When you first heard the news from the Pulitzer Committee, what were you thinking right then?" Snyder asked.

"What was I thinking right then? I was in a transcendent mood of such triumph for someone who suffered so much during his life! You see, he was so brilliant that, when he was in grammar school, I had to fight twice to have him transferred to another grade, and they fought me, and I was out in the hall with the principal, and his first grade teacher said, 'He's a different child. You can't stifle that mind. You have to give him a chance,' so when he was six, he entered the second grade, and then when he was in fourth grade, he skipped the fourth grade and went into the fifth. . . . Now, he was tall for his age, sturdy, and he developed into a football-type physique. That saved him, because if the darling had been puny and bespectacled, the other boys might have been pummeling him. Am I right?"

By this point, Thelma had both Snyder and the audience in the palm of her hand.

"A smart young man, huh?" asked Snyder.

Thelma glared at him. "A scholarly genius! Tom, you're putting it too mildly!"

Snyder attempted another question, but Thelma cut him off. "Now listen to me, Tom. I told you when I met you, I'm Irish." Snyder made another attempt to say something, but once again, Thelma interrupted. "Someone," she said with great authority, "told me that in Ireland perception extends to the working classes!"

A man in the audience shouted out, "That's right!"

"That's beautiful," Thelma continued. "The Irish *are* perceptive, the most perceptive nation in the world! Maybe East Indians are," she mused. "I don't know any East Indians."

Snyder, slightly rattled, quickly cut in again, "We will continue with Mrs. O'Toole right after these announcements. Let me do these little commercials now, and we'll be right back."

Thelma drew up in her chair. "I don't think I can spare the time!"

"Oh, yes you can," Snyder said, and broke to commercials.

In the second half of the interview, in a discussion of her struggle to get the book published, after prodding by Snyder, Thelma revealed that it was an editor from W.W. Norton who told her that "the book has literary style, but comic novels don't sell!" She went into more detail about how she had given the book to Walker Percy and how he had been instrumental in getting it published. "Walker is the guiding light and master of this great project that has brought such honor to the city of New Orleans and the State of Louisiana."

"Not to mention the good family Toole, who dwell therein, huh?" said Snyder.

When we left the studio, we were set upon by a small band of autograph seekers. It occurred to me that they probably had no idea who Thelma was, but were here every night collecting the autographs of whoever happened to be on the show. Thelma graciously obliged them. She was now a bona fide celebrity and they were her fans!

From Rockefeller Center, we were driven to the Warwick Hotel where Barney Rosset, head of Grove Press, had arranged a reception. Thelma, in her element, held court. She autographed copies of the new paperback edition of *Confederacy,* played the piano and sang, and did her interpretations of various characters in the book. It was a role she had learned to perfection in New Orleans in the months following the first appearance of the book. Among those at the reception was Ken's old friend Nicholas Polites, now an architectural writer living in New York. After the reception, which was mainly for the press, Rosset invited about a dozen people to have dinner with him back at the Berkshire Place. By the time we had finished eating, it was almost time for the show to be broadcast. Thelma and I went up to her room and watched it. She agreed with my opinion that she had been superb.

In early June, I accompanied Thelma on another trip to promote the book. We flew to Toronto where she was invited to appear on *Canada A.M.* As in New York, we were put up in a luxurious hotel, the Park Plaza, which was comfortable, but stuffy and pretentious. The evening we arrived, we dined on bad, expensive food in the lugubrious hotel dining room, and Thelma then went to her room to bed for her appearance was scheduled for very early the next morning.

On the live broadcast of *Canada A.M.,* Thelma was immediately preceded by the British author, Hugo Vickers, who was interviewed about his recent book on Prince Charles and Princess Diana. In my journal, I described Vickers as "an overly-refined young man with beautiful eyelashes and manners." He spoke softly and was very starry-eyed about the Royal Wedding. When he finished he left behind him a mood of breathless gentility.

It was soon shattered by Thelma. One of the first questions she was asked by the interviewer, Norm Perry, was what precisely Robert Gottlieb had told Ken when he finally rejected *Confederacy?*

"He told him," said Thelma, her eyes wide with outrage, "that Myrna Minkoff was a *pain* in the *ass!*" Mr. Perry almost fell out of his chair. "Now I ask you," Thelma continued, "is that any kind of language for an educated man to use?"

CHAPTER EIGHT
Anatomy of a Rejection

On the plane to Toronto, Thelma gave me copies of the correspondence between Ken and Simon and Schuster, which I then read for the first time. Thelma had just got the letters, or at least copies of them, back from Rhoda Faust, owner of the Maple Street Book Shop, with whom Thelma would be doing battle for the rest of her life (more of this story later). The letters detail most of the history of Ken's initial encouragement from Robert Gottlieb, who was then an editor at Simon and Schuster, and the ultimate rejection of his novel. They are fascinating reading.

The first letter, dated June 9, 1964, is from Robert Gottlieb's assistant, Jean Jollet, who informs Ken that Gottlieb will probably not be able to see Ken on a visit he planned to New York because Gottlieb will be leaving for Europe. She finishes the letter by writing, "Is now the time for me to tell you that I laughed, chortled, collapsed my way through Confederacy?" That certainly must have been heartening to the young author.

A week later, Gottlieb himself wrote to Ken, expressing regret that he would be away while Ken was in New York.

He wrote of the "major problem" of the book:

> Not only do the various threads need resolving; they can always be tied together conveniently. What must happen is that they must be strong and meaningful all the way through—not merely episodically and then wittily pulled together to make everything look as if it's come out right. In other words, there must be a point to everything you have in the book, a real point, not just amusingness that's forced to figure itself out.

Ken did go to New York that June, did drop by to see Gottlieb's assistant, and then returned to New Orleans to work on revising *Confederacy.*

On December 14 of that same year, Gottlieb wrote Ken again:

> In many ways I think you've done an excellent job— of pulling the plot together, of making sense of certain non-sense things, of strengthening certain characters, of eliminating others. The book is much better. It is still not right.

Gottlieb then wrote that he had discussed *Confederacy* with the person he calls "probably the best literary agent in town," Candida Donadio, who at that time was handling Joseph Heller, Bruce Jay Friedman, John Cheever, Nelson Algren, to name but a few of the celebrated American writers in her stable. "What we think is this. That you are wildly funny often, funnier than almost anyone else around, and our kind of funny . . . " But he concludes of Ken's book that:

it isn't really about anything. And that's something no one can do anything about. Certainly an editor can't say: "Put meaning in."

Which is all very well, but what to do. The book could be improved and published. But it wouldn't succeed; we could never say that it was anything.

The letter must have been a blow, but Ken replied in a brief letter that revealed little of his true feelings. "Ironically, I found your letter encouraging," Ken wrote. "Perhaps this sounds masochistic; however, I'm grateful for the attention you've given the book." A month later, on January 15, 1965, Ken wrote Gottlieb, "The only sensible thing to do, it seems to me, is to ask for the manuscript. Aside from some deletions, I don't think I could really do much to the book now—and, of course, even with revisions you might not be satisfied."

Gottlieb evidently did return the manuscript to Ken, and in early March of that year, they must have had a last telephone conversation about the book. On March 3, Ken, uncharacteristically, put his desperation in a letter to Gottlieb:

> I've been trying to think straight since speaking with you on the telephone, but confusion and depression have immobilized my mind. I have to come out of this, though, or I'll never do anything. Writing a letter might be a good beginning. It may be long. If I had been less inarticulate when speaking with you, all of this might not have been necessary. Perhaps this is the letter I should have written you in December rather

than that brief stiff-upper-lip of a note that only served to prolong things.

After the telephone conversation, I was certain that I was simply hanging on by overeager fingernails. Perhaps I still am. When it was suggested that I write another book if I could, I felt that you were offering me an opening to withdraw with at least a little grace. My feeling might have been accurate.

Whenever I attempt to talk in connection with Confederacy of Dunces, I become anxious and inarticulate. I feel very paternal about the book; the feeling is actually androgynous because I feel as if I gave birth to it, too. I know that it has flaws, yet I am afraid that some stranger will bring them to my attention. The worse example of this was my apprehensive, incoherent meeting with Miss Jollet during which I, bent with obsequious-ness, almost sank through the floor in between my silences, cryptic comments, and occasional mindless (for it had left me) absurdities. I didn't fare much better on the phone. But one or two of the few things that I did say seem to have been misinterpreted (which, in view of their source, is understandable). A question follows, I guess: why did I want to drop in to Simon and Schuster, why did I ask you to call me? At any rate, this reticence on my part has succeeded in my being confused, which is ironic. I'm not given to discussing myself, but I have to say some things.

Ken then goes on to give a history of how the book began in 1961 while he was teaching at Hunter and doing part-time doctoral work at Columbia. He was, he writes " . . . in the frustrating cycle of someone who wants to write, has decided to teach, and must get a Ph.D. to do anything decent academically." He mentions that in the summer of 1961 he had time to work on an earlier version of the book "in which Ignatius was called Humphrey Wildblood."

Ken tells Gottlieb how he was drafted into the army and given the assignment in Puerto Rico, which finally gave him time and a private space to work on the book. When the time came for his release from the army, he writes, "I had completed more than half of the book, and, as opposed to my earlier writing, I could re-read what I had done without feeling painfully embarrassed." He writes of his decision to abandon New York and get a job at "a carefully selected, small, quiet local college where, as I had hoped, there's little demand on time and almost none on mind."

> The book went along until President Kennedy's assassination. Then I couldn't write anything more. Nothing seemed funny to me. I went into a funk. At last, in February of '64, with no changes and revisions, I typed up what I had, briefly concluded it, and began sending it around in the hope that someone might take an interest in it.
>
> That brings me up to your first reading of the book (though perhaps you've stopped reading this letter) . . . The book is not autobiography; neither is it altogether invention. While the plot is manipulation and juxtaposition of characters, with one or two exceptions the people and places in the book are drawn from observation and experience. I am not in the book; I've never pretended to be. But I am writing about things that I know, and in recounting these, it's difficult not to feel them.

In the revision plot threads were tied together, but sometimes this turned out to be only sound and fury. Myrna turned into a cartoon in a book where almost everyone else was basically real, but she was supposed to be very, very likable; if, to an objective reader, she is a "pain in the ass," then she's a debacle. But when I sent you the revision I was certain that the Levys were the book's worst flaw. In trying to make them "plot" characters, they got out of hand, becoming worse and worse, and turned into cardboard whose conversations I was embarrassed to re-read . . . but Irene Reilly, Santa Battaglia, Patrolman Mancuso . . . these people say something about New Orleans. They're real as individuals and also as representative of a group. One night recently I watched again as Santa bumped around while Irene sat on a couch guffawing into a drink. And how many times have I seen Santa kissing her mother's picture. Burma Jones is not a fantasy, and neither is Miss Trixie and her job, the Night of Joy Club, and so on. There's no need to burden you with an itemized list.

In short, little of the book is invented; the plot certainly is. It's true that in the unreality of my Puerto Rican experience, this book became more real to me than what was happening around me; I was beginning to talk and act like Ignatius. No doubt this is why there's so much of him and why his verbosity becomes tiring. It's really not his verbosity but mine. And the book, begun one Sunday afternoon, became a way of life. With Ignatius as an agent, my New Orleans experiences began to fit in, one after the other, and then I was simply observing and not inventing. . . .

When I received your letter in December, I was both

encouraged and discouraged. I was encouraged by the kind comments, the indications of continued interest, and very discouraged by "The book could be improved and published, but it wouldn't succeed." . . . The telephone call turned my doubts into despair. The book seemed to have become nothing. I could only ask that it be returned so that I wouldn't appear too greatly unaware. I was very confused by the telephone call; the letter you wrote me after I requested the manuscript confused me more. I feel now somewhat like a bouncing ball . . . and much of this stems from my own silent apprehension whenever I must discuss the book. . . .

You mentioned Bruce Jay Friedman on the phone in an oblique connection with this book, Stern is my favorite modern novel; I had an intense personal reaction to the book; I love it. As a matter of fact, it was after reading Stern that I mailed this book to Simon and Schuster; I even copied your address from Stern. If I could put myself as humanly as he does, I'd try. Since I liked Stern so greatly, I thought that whoever published it might like my book; while I was blacking out in Miss Jollett's presence, I managed to convey this news by one or two non sequitars [sic] that climaxed that eventful visit.

But this book is what I know, what I've seen and experienced. I can't throw these people away. No one has ever done much insofar as writing about this milieu is concerned, I don't think. Myrna and the Levys may only serve to hinder the book, especially in their being extraneous. If the Levys caused me such problems, they don't belong. I certainly did not feel the Levys. What was very accurate in your commentary about the revision was your separating real and unreal characters.

In other words, I'm going to work on the book again. I haven't even been able to look at the manuscript since I got it back, but since something like 50 percent of my soul is in the thing, I can't let it rot without trying. And I don't think I could write anything else until this is given at least another chance.

Gottlieb replied to Ken's *cri de coeur* about three weeks later. The delay, he said, was "partly because I'm not sure what to say, partly because I've been looking for a time when I could write something un-frantic and relatively thought out." He mentions "work, civil rights activities, and the accumulated psychic garbage and practical frenzy of one's private life," as other reasons for his slow response to Ken's letter.

I can't say much sensible to you about your mortifications over your performance on the telephone with me, or here in the office with Jean Jollett. Six years of analysis haven't robbed me of my own brand of insecurities or neurosis, and why should I try to rob you of yours? But remember that if to you, we are threatening figures in a complicated and confusing world, to us you are an attractive and important mystery. You don't have to put yourself on the line in person, since you're [sic] done your job on paper; we are the ones who have to appear and behave strongly and well. Besides, silence never seems frantic—it didn't occur to me that you were anything but cautious and relatively easy about accepting criticism from a total stranger.

I'm glad you wrote all you did about your history. First of all, curiosity is satisfied, then it means that we have a connection, since you wouldn't have talked that way to an un-connection. Just as I liked your book, I like your letter—which means I like you. Which means a possibility of friendship—which is good. Of course, you don't know me, since you haven't had the advantage of reading a novel of mine. (I haven't written one). You must take me on faith, while I have living proof of your you-ness.

About the book. Everything you write about it makes sense to me, including your doubts, and your ultimate determinations. Since we agree on what is real and what isn't, there's not much point to recounting the areas I approve of and disapprove of. You know, and you knew them before I mentioned them. As you explain yourself, I see that it is essential that you work on into the book, and I'm glad you are. My words—"it wouldn't succeed"—I can't tell you now what I meant by them. Probably that the book as it stood wouldn't sell. But the trouble is—and always is—that when someone like yourself is living off from the center of cultural-business activities, with only a thin lifeline to that center, through vague and solitary contacts, everything gets disproportionate, difficult to analyze, to give proper weight to.

It is like those odd people who turn up in New Zealand or Tanganyika or Finland, writing or painting masterpieces. They have their own power, but they read or look as if the artist has had to discover the forms for himself. They don't have the assurance of worldliness and mutual interest and energy with others. So I can see that to you I (or Jean) is not merely a person, but a voice with more authority that it could possibly deserve. Not that I'm not good at my job, because I am and no one is better; but that I'm just someone, and a good deal less talented than you.

I don't know just what I've said here, and I don't know that I want to turn back to see (a Lot's wife complex). What I want basically to have said is this: You have nothing to apologize about; you are a good writer and a serious person and are doing your job seriously and modestly and of course it isn't easy. As for the actual rewrite, I tell you as I may have already told you, "I will never abandon Mr. Micawber." A writer's decisions are his own, not his editor's. If you know you have to continue with Ignatius, that is of course what you should do. I will read, reread, edit, perhaps publish, generally cope, until you are fed up with me. What more can I say?

Please write me short or long at any time, if only to say that you're working (or not). Or if you like, show me bits of what you've done. Or don't; whichever would be more useful. Cheer up. Work. We are overcoming. Best, Bob Gottlieb.

Five days later, Ken replied:

That was a calming letter, and I appreciated it.

In that it was an unburdening, my letter to you was itself a relief—as unburdenings are. I had to talk; thanks for having listened. I had lost perspective on the book and on myself, too. But basically I have a sense of the ridiculous and of the absurd (including my own absurdities) which keeps me afloat.

What happened, I think, was this: ten years of suppressed feeling surfaced when I first heard from you about this book. In 1954, when I was sixteen, I wrote a

book called The Neon Bible, a grim, adolescent socio-
logical attack upon the hatreds spawned by the various
Calvinist religions in the South—and the fundamental-
ist mentality is one of the roots of what has been happening in Alabama, etc. The book, of course, was bad,
but I sent it off a couple of times anyway. After that I
wrote pieces and beginnings that were never inflicted
upon any editor. For one thing, my mind was diverted
during those years by other things. Then, as I wrote,
with Puerto Rico there came a physical and mental
detachment, and the relatively unused energies of
almost ten years came flooding into this book and created too great a concentration of emotion. Had I been
submitting things regularly during those years, I might
have received some editorial comments and suggestions
that might have provided me with some degree or perspective or at least a little "cool."

I've been re-reading the book. What is most apparent is the need for a red pencil through a lot of it. There
are hints in the book of developing themes and ideas,
but they seem to be abandoned before they become con-
sistent statements. I see a possibility of having the book
say something that will be real, that will develop out of
the characters themselves and what I know of them, that
will not simply be a superficial imposition of "purpose."
The book as it is evades certain logical consequences of
the nature of the characters themselves, and in this way
wastes a character or two. But I do have ideas for the
book, and I am beginning to work on it. I hope that I'll
be able to send you a re-working of the thing in the not
too distant future; since I am able to "see" and "hear"
these characters, I can always work with them.

We'll see what happens . . .

And I have rallied, have begun to work. And spring is here.

This is the last of the extant letters from Ken to Gottlieb. It is dated March 28, 1965, almost four years to the day before Ken was to commit suicide in Biloxi. There must have been another letter, of which no copy exists, for on January 17, 1966, Gottlieb wrote a final letter to Ken:

Dear Mr. Toole,

I was glad to hear from you, particularly since a week or two ago—when the year changed—I had wondered how you were coming along. My interest in the book remains what it was. I liked a lot of it a lot; thought it needed much work; and have a small doubt that something so long agonized over is ever going to live up to (at least) your own expectations. I certainly want to read it again, when you're through doing what you're doing.

I don't think your purpose in writing me was vague. Everyone needs to feel outside, professional interest in what he's doing; we live on it. But you are not working in a void, even as far as New York publishing is concerned: at least this one editor is interested. And hoping that you've made the right choice in continuing with this book rather than starting something new. But that decision has been made; now to see what you do with it. Onwards. Best, Bob Gottlieb

I have quoted extensively from the correspondence because I felt paraphrase might have been unfair to both Ken and Gottlieb. The story, in Thelma's angry version, has always been oversimplified. She told things as she saw them, and in her view Gottlieb was simply the cruel ogre who had destroyed her son. The letters show that he continued to be extremely interested in and sympathetic to Ken and to give him what he considered good advice. Far from abandoning Ken, Gottlieb was one of the first to recognize his genius, and the decision to break off the relationship was Ken's, not Gottlieb's. Robert Gottlieb went on to play a major role in the world of American editing. After he left Simon and Schuster he became president of Knopf, and later editor of the *New Yorker.* Thelma's portrayal of him as an insensitive, heartless villain who single-handedly destroyed her son, which has become an integral part of the *Confederacy* myth, is grossly unfair, as the above letters clearly show.

Reading these letters on the plane, I realized that what had been published was probably Ken's first draft of the book, before he undertook the revisions suggested by Gottlieb. I asked Thelma about it. She replied that the published form of *Confederacy* was indeed the un-revised first draft. "You should have seen the revisions! Like this!" indicating several inches with her thumb and finger. "I discarded it," she said, referring to the revised manuscript. "I was so distraught after Ken's death—and at first I didn't want it to be published because I knew they would bring up the suicide. Suicide taints the whole family, you know. I didn't want them to bring up the suicide, so I discarded it. Then, as time passed, I realized that it *had* to be published."

I asked Thelma if a revised copy of the book might still be in one of the boxes of Ken's belongings. "Maybe," she said. "I think the only things I destroyed were the suicide note and the rejection slips." "Could we look for it?" I asked. She agreed. I hoped that there still existed a later version of the book, another manuscript that showed Gottlieb's editorial guidance and Ken's reworking, perhaps an even better novel than the published one.

Some weeks after we got back from Toronto, I drove over to New Orleans to help Thelma look through boxes that she said held some of Ken's belongings. I was there, as requested, about 8 A.M., but we waited until her brother Arthur left the house to do errands. Thelma didn't want him to know what we were up to. After we heard the back door slam, we went into a room off the kitchen. It was almost completely filled with cardboard boxes, in one of which might be the revised manuscript. I went through them all, but found only neatly folded paper grocery bags and hoardings of small gift boxes within larger ones. And there were many of Arthur's dress shirts that had never been taken out of their cellophane. But there was no trace of the manuscript. I did find Arthur's typewriter and a folder of the verse he had written for special occasions at the Standard Fruit Company, his employer of many years. "Oh, yes, Arthur's clever," Thelma said. "The Ducoing intelligence. He was the *Poet Laureate* of Standard Fruit, you know!" Her voice was heavy with sarcasm.

Thelma did not really seem surprised to hear that there were none of Ken's papers in the back room. When I told her what I had and had not found she asked me to see if there were still linens in a chest the cover of which was weighed down with cardboard boxes. I managed to pry the lid up enough to get a hand in and felt that the linens were still there, assured her that they were. Just then we heard Arthur returning, and that was the end of the search. Thelma went into her bedroom and came back with a pair of stainless steel toenail clippers. "These were Ken's, honey," she told me. "I want you to have them!" She handed them to me as if they were some kind of bizarre consolation prize.

CHAPTER NINE
A Saturday with Thelma

The evening before my fruitless search for the revised manuscript of *Confederacy,* Thelma had been invited to dinner by one of her new admirers, the Consul General of Argentina, Adolfo Saracho. The party was on board the *Punta Norte,* an Argentinean ship docked in New Orleans. Because the gangway up to the quarter-deck had proved too steep for her to ascend, she had been hoisted on board with a crane. The party made the society page of the New Orleans *Times-Picayune,* where Thelma was called "the new darling of the party line." The *Lagniappe* column mentioned that the other guests included the head of the New Orleans World's Fair, the director and other members of the Dock Board, and a prominent lawyer whose wife was with the Tourist Commission. John Geiser, a childhood friend of Ken, was Thelma's escort. Thelma was moving more and more frequently in New Orleans's high social circles, which she had always viewed with resentment from the outside.

Thelma said she had greatly enjoyed the attentions of the Consul General, the ship's captain, and the other guests. The food, she told me, had been almost inedible, but that had not stopped her from bringing home a sizable portion of leftovers: a half-dozen thick slices of beef and some sausages. It was to be the principal component of our lunch that day, although she had also made some tuna-fish salad, just in case the beef and sausages were still inedible after she had boiled them for several hours. With lots of Creole mustard, the Argentine leftovers were actually quite tasty, but I was not sure how long they and the tuna salad had been sitting in her hot kitchen, and I wondered if we were going to be ill.

Before lunch, I crossed Elysian Fields to Schwegmann's supermarket, an institution peculiar to New Orleans, to buy Thelma the frozen strawberries she loved. I had never been to Schwegmann's on a Saturday before. The ambiance was pure *Confederacy*. The store was filled with a collection of mostly unwashed grotesques of all colors, sizes, and shapes doing their weekend shopping. There were many elderly and bowed, poorly dressed men and women fighting their way through the too-narrow aisles with shopping carts. An angry-looking young Latin-type in a blue undershirt and tight jeans was aggressively pricing cans of Crisco with a labeling pistol. Young black dudes were bopping around. A tiny old lady in a dusty velvet coat and matching hat was resolutely trying to cut into the checkout line, ignoring the dirty looks and rude remarks. A wan, skinny, effete young man with his shirt unbuttoned down to his scruffy navel was standing in line holding a single can of cat food. Above the whir of the air conditioning, the Irish-Channel accent could be heard loud and sometimes clear.

After consuming the dubious meat and tuna salad and

the semi-defrosted strawberries, Thelma and I got into my car, the air-conditioning of which had just stopped working. It was not a comfortable place to be on a July day in New Orleans, but we had a heavy schedule ahead of us.

Thelma had several errands to run, and we were invited to an afternoon party given by another one of Thelma's new admirers, a young man named Rick who lived in an apartment complex in Metairie. We picked up David Swoyer, a curator at the New Orleans Museum of Art and one of my close friends, at the Milan Street house of his boss, John Bullard, director of the museum and also a friend. We arrived about one o'clock, and John invited us to join them for lunch at the Pontchartrain Hotel. Since we had just finished a large and possibly lethal meal, we declined the invitation to eat, but sat with John and David in the deliciously air-conditioned coffee shop of the hotel, a real treat after an hour in my baking car. Thelma put on her usual performance for the benefit of John, whom she had not met before. He seemed entranced.

From the Pontchartrain, we went to the Swiss Bakery on Magazine Street and I went in to get, as instructed by Thelma, the $3.95 "fancy mix" of pastries, which was to be our contribution to the party at Rick's. (I remembered Irene Reilly, in the first chapter of *Confederacy,* going to the bakery department of D. H. Holmes to buy "two dozen of them fancy mix," and the "German on Magazine Street" where she buys jelly doughnuts for Ignatius. This must have been the place.) Then we went to the French Quarter to pick up Russell Rocke, the impresario of the Toulouse Theater and the producer of the jazz musical *One Mo' Time,* currently enjoying a very successful run at the Toulouse. I noted in my journal that Rocke was

> quick-minded, fast talking, looks like a fox, a sly brown fox, wants very badly to get his hands on *Neon Bible,* publish it, make a film of it, be Thelma's agent. He was wearing a chic, un-pressed linen suit and carrying a purse. Very New York, not very New Orleans. He has a French girlfriend named Martine whom we did not meet because Thelma does not like her and did not invite her.

Thelma seldom liked her men's lady friends.

As I recall, our host that afternoon, Rick, worked in a record store. I don't know where Thelma had met him. Probably at a book signing. He and his roommate lived in a small, neat apartment in an un-chic part of Metairie. The party consisted of Thelma, me, David, Russell, Rick, and Rick's roommate, about whom I remember nothing at all. We drank cheap champagne and ate the sickly-sweet pastries. Rick had an upright piano with an electric attachment. He played ragtime. Thelma played and sang show tunes. And then the piano, with the help of the electric attachment, played by itself. Russell looked very bored and impatient. David and I, who had been up since very early that morning, nearly dozed off several times. At five o'clock we headed back to New Orleans. As we were leaving the parking lot of the apartment complex, Thelma made some remark that let me know she had not been very impressed with the party or with our host. The setting was a far cry from the glamorous venue of the evening before. "Must be kind of sad living way out here in place like this," she said.

After we dropped off Russell Rocke at his theater, we went to the levee by the old Jax Brewery building off Jackson Square and prepared to board the paddle-wheeler *Natchez* for an evening cruise. It was Thelma's idea and Thelma's treat. A steep gangway went up to the boat, and I was very grateful that David was along to help because this time there was no crane for Thelma. We were early and were pre-boarded by a handsome, café-au-lait colored attendant in a slightly less than spiffy uniform. There were already hordes of un-savory looking tourists on board, but we found good seats by the front railing, overlooking the prow. The whistle blew, blasting our eardrums, and the *Natchez* eased away from the dock for a very smooth cruise toward the Chalmette Battlefield where Thelma's ancestor, Jean Baptiste Ducoing, had been a gunner in the Battle of New Orleans in 1815. Just past Chalmette, we turned and went close to a file of rusty ships at anchor. One of them was a freighter from the Cayman Islands. A swarm of half-naked black men were lolling on its deck and as we went by they jumped up and down and waved excitedly. The ship went back upstream passing warehouses, then the trees of Jackson Square, and the tall steeple of the St. Louis Cathedral. We continued under the bridge beyond the uptown wharves. It was too early for moonlight, but as we turned a second time and headed back to the mooring, the sky began to darken and the lights in the hotels and other buildings began to come on. "What a beautiful cruise," said Thelma. "So soothing!" Uncharacteristically, she had spoken very little as we glided up and down the river, apparently deep in thought, or perhaps she was just a little tired.

We were all hungry and Thelma said she felt like eating fried oysters. David suggested that we go to La Péniche, the funky little restaurant in the Faubourg Marigny where he and I had eaten breakfast that morning, where we often ate breakfast when I was in New Orleans. The early morning crowd was usually made up of two distinct groups: the dazed-looking, sometimes drunk, all-nighters who were making their final stop before crashing, and a table or two of bright-eyed policemen who were just beginning their day. The former lent an air of pleasant decadence; the latter a sense of safety. The food was fairly good and the prices were moderate. There seemed to be a high rate of turnover among the waiters who were usually young and inexperienced, but generally agreeable, sometimes even witty.

The evening crowd, which was not much of one, was less distinctive. Thelma ordered a fried oyster sandwich on plain toast. "Not bad," she said without much expression. "Different. They've never heard of cornmeal. Used white flour, but not bad." David and I both had red-bean burgers which appeared disgusting, but were delicious. Our waiter, who looked and moved more like a basketball player than a waiter, told us he was from Ohio and that this was his first day on the job. When I went up to the counter to pay the bill, he asked me if Thelma were my mother. "No," I said, and explained who she was. "Wow!' he said. "No kidding! I just read the book!" He stared at her instead of at the cash register while he was making change, but managed to give me back precisely the amount I was due.

CHAPTER TEN

Doonie

In his *Times-Picayune* article about Ken and Thelma, Dalt Wonk writes of a love interest in Ken's life: Ruth Lafrantz, a coed from Mississippi Ken had met on a blind date. According to Wonk, Ken and Lafrantz realized that they had a lot in common and began dating. Ken even introduced her to Thelma, who, not surprisingly, did not approve. Ken and Lafrantz both applied to and were accepted by Columbia University graduate school in 1957 and continued seeing each other in New York. Ken is said to have proposed to Lafrantz, but she equivocated, and eventually became engaged to someone else. She is quoted as saying of Ken "Our relationship was light, not heavy—light, but profound." Was that a way of saying that it was platonic? At any rate, Lafrantz seems to have decided that Ken was not a good prospect for marriage.

Another woman with whom Ken has been linked is Emilie "Russ" Dietrich Griffin. They had known each other slightly in New Orleans when Ken was studying English at Tulane and Dietrich was studying English at Newcomb and both were working on the Tulane-Newcomb newspaper,

The Hullabaloo. Their friendship developed when they moved to New York. While Ken was studying at Columbia and teaching at Hunter, Dietrich was working for an advertising agency. They dated, wrote Dietrich in a memoir she published in *Image: A Journal of the Arts & Religion,* but " . . . it was never exactly a romance." Ken, she wrote, was a terrific dancer and lots of fun to be with, and they made joyful excursions together to Roseland Dance City and the Apollo Theater in Harlem to see "Moms" Mabley. Like his relationship with Lafrantz, his connection to Dietrich seems to have been "light, not heavy."

As far as I recall, Ken never mentioned Ruth Lafrantz or Russ Dietrich to me, nor did he speak of any romantic attachments. His sexuality, as far as I could tell, was not something he wanted to talk to me about. He gave me the impression that he was not very interested in the subject, but perhaps that was a smokescreen. Nicholas Polites, who knew Ken longer and better than I did, thinks that there was at one time something sexual between Ken and his close friend, Doonie Guibet. He says he remembers Ken telling him something about it. If there was something sexual between the two boys, it could have been nothing more than youthful experimentation. Nicholas also recalls taking Ken to a party in the French Quarter that may have been the inspiration for the gay party scene in *Confederacy.* Nicholas said that Ken's reaction to it was extremely negative.

With Nicholas and with me, Ken was very reticent about his sexuality, as he was about many aspects of his life. In the interview that Bobby Byrne gave Carmine Palumbo, he said that Ken "kept his own counsel," that he had no confidant. My impression was the same. If Ken was gay, he did not want it to be generally known, not a surprising attitude in those closeted and circumspect years.

There is also evidence that Ken did feel a sexual attraction to women. When Ken and Nicholas Polites were both on the English faculty at Southwestern, Nicholas remembers that Ken often expressed his sexual interest in Patricia Rickels in very crude terms. Patricia was then young, extremely bright, vivacious, and witty. I recently asked Patricia if she were aware that Ken had been attracted physically to her. She replied that at that time she was very happily married and devoted to her husband, Milton, and that, also being very innocent, she was completely oblivious of any sexual overtones in the attention that Ken paid her. She said that Milton, however, did not like it and got a little fed up with Ken. Pat said it never occurred to her that Ken might have been homosexual. She felt that his interests were definitely heterosexual, but that he was very shy and inexperienced. She noticed that he seemed very drawn to Ann Ward, the very beautiful young wife of Jack Ward, the Henry James specialist on the Southwestern faculty, and thought the attraction must have been at least partly physical.

There exists in the Toole archive at Tulane a letter from a woman named "Ellen" whom Ken must have known in New York, and who evidently felt passionately about him. The letter, which is dated June 2, but with no indication of the year, begins "I took my last exam today, followed it with a voice lesson 'chaser,' and then found your letter waiting for me, as effective as a Soma holiday!" (Soma was the drug that replaced religion and with which people controlled their anxieties in Aldous Huxley's novel about a utopian future, *Brave New World.*)

Ellen tells Ken about her activities: "reading, sunning and playing a terrible game of tennis at Sebago Beach" (in Harriman State Park, just north of New York City), mentions her cousin Henry's birthday, and warns Ken that her mother may be sending him a loaf of rye bread. "She misses serving dinner to you, but not possibly as much as I miss being with you. I love you, I love you, I love you. Ellen." There is a P.S. about a package, which presumably Ken sent her, but has not yet arrived. "I can hardly wait. My love to you, darling."

From the one-sided evidence it sounds like his relationship to Ellen was much less platonic that those he had with Ruth Lafrantz and Russ Dietrich. Perhaps, since the relationship took place in New York away from Thelma's eyes, Ken was able to relax into a more normal relationship with someone of the opposite sex. But since no evidence exists to show how passionately Ken felt in return, this can only be speculation.

Shortly after my return from Toronto in June of 1981, I happened to pick up a copy of the New Orleans *Times Picayune/States Item,* a paper I seldom read. I noticed an article with the headline: "Orleans Man Is Held In Roommate's Killing." The photograph that accompanied the article showed a detective leading away a handcuffed man with a droopy mustache, his hair disheveled and his shirt tail out. Out of mild curiosity I read the article, which at first rang no bells. It concerned a man named Lowry

Guibet, aged forty-three, who was being held on a charge of murdering his roommate in their apartment on Polymnia Street. The dead man was one Peter Ducos, aged thirty, identified as a waiter at the Holiday Inn on Royal Street. The police reported that Guibet claimed that when he was awakened by a knock on the door shortly after 4 A.M., he opened it and Ducos stumbled in saying he had been shot. But the detectives said they found signs of a probable struggle in the apartment, and learned from neighbors that Ducos and Guibet had had fights during the days that preceded the killing. Guibet was booked with murder.

Halfway through the article, a bell did ring. Could Lowry Guibet be Doonie Guibet, Ken's friend? The photograph bore little resemblance to the pretty boy I had briefly met a quarter of a century before.

When I next saw Thelma, I asked her if Doonie's real name was Lowry. She said yes, it was, and I told her about the article describing Guibet's arrest for murder. She did not seem surprised, and then related what I already knew, that Doonie and Ken had been great friends for many years.

They used to have a good time together. He was such a handsome boy. They went to see Mae West when she was doing a show here, and I remember their laughing and going backstage to get her autograph. When they were young they were inseparable. Then Doonie moved to New York. Ken went to see him in his apartment there once. He mentioned a large picture of a boy. I don't remember if it was a nude boy or not, but Ken didn't like what Doonie was doing with his life, and eventually he broke with him.

When I had first looked up Thelma on Elysian Fields Avenue, she mentioned Doonie and told me she had saved the letters he had written Ken, but those letters were not with the gift she made of Ken's papers to Tulane. Perhaps his arrest for murder had persuaded her that Doonie was not someone she wanted Ken's name associated with. When Ken was a child, Thelma decided which children were worthy to be his friends. It seems likely that she also chose which of Ken's friends were to be remembered as close to him after his death.

Dorian Greene, the elegant young man in the bottle-green velvet jacket whom Ignatius and Mrs. Reilly meet in the Night of Joy bar, is an exaggerated but stereotypical gay man, and one of the least sympathetic characters in the book. It seems likely that Dorian Greene was modeled on Doonie Guibet. As Ken wrote Gottlieb, he was "simply observing, not inventing." There is not only the obvious association of the character's name with Oscar Wilde's monster of depravity, Dorian Gray, but also a great similarity between the sounds of Doonie Guibet and Dorian Gray, a coincidence that must have struck Ken and amused him.

The unflattering portrayal of Dorian Greene is more than just tinged with homophobia, and homophobia, both externalized and internalized, is not an uncommon phenomenon among gay men who have not come to terms with their sexuality. It seems to me that a struggle with his sexual identity might have been another of the causes of Ken's despair, and perhaps also accounts for the jaundiced view of gay life in his novel. But I accept the fact that I will never know for sure whether Ken was gay or straight or something in between.

CHAPTER ELEVEN

The Robert Coles Lecture

Maurice duQuesnay, a professor of English at the University of Southwestern Louisiana, telephoned me in August of 1981 to ask for Thelma's telephone number so that he could invite her to a lecture, a psychoanalytic interpretation of *Confederacy* by Harvard professor and writer Robert Coles. I made a practice of not giving out Thelma's telephone number, so I gave him her address and suggested that he write her.

I knew Maurice slightly and by reputation as another eccentric type. Born in New Orleans, he had studied at Marquette University and had at one time planned to become a Jesuit priest, but after a stormy exit from the Catholic church (rumor had it that he had tried to throw a Jesuit down an elevator shaft), had converted to Judaism. Maurice had learned Hebrew and taught it at the synagogue in Lafayette. It was there he met and became friendly with Flora Levy, an elderly spinster from a prominent Lafayette Jewish family. Flora had quietly worked her way up to a very responsible position at the First National Bank of Lafayette, and decided before she died to leave her considerable estate to the USL Foundation to sponsor a lecture series. The money came with the stipulation that Maurice administer the funds, and he thus became the permanent chairman of the Flora Levy Lecture Committee, a position which gave him a certain power within the university.

Maurice was known among his colleagues as a prickly and volatile personality. A friend in the USL English department told me that he had caused an unpleasant stir on the occasion of the first Levy lecture, given by Isaac Bashevis Singer, when his guest list for the reception included two local firemen but omitted the head of the USL English department.

I wrote to Thelma telling her that Maurice would be in touch, and advised caution in getting involved with him. But I needn't have bothered. Maurice's arrangements for the Coles lecture and the reception after it were, as far as I know, uncontroversial and everything went smoothly. And Maurice was a big hit with Thelma. "I think I'm going to kidnap him," she told me after their first meeting. "He's so entertaining, that vibrating mass of double martinis!"

The lecture, *Gravity and Grace in the Novel A Confederacy of Dunces,* was delivered in an auditorium of the USL campus on September 18, 1981. It was well attended and appreciatively received. In a short and eloquent lecture, Coles invoked the writings of Simone Weil and her stressing of "gravity and grace." Gravity, he said was the "everpresent 'weight' of our minds and bodies," and grace "an unexpected, a mysterious, an utterly providential arrival: Him." His eloquence was such that no one seemed startled by his comparing Ignatius to the Roman Catholic Church, which, he said, "like Ignatius, had to keep trying, keep reaching out to the entire arc of humanity, keep hoping in various ways to become a spiritual instrument in the lives of every possible kind of person, as Ignatius for all his absurdities and tics and postures and excesses manages to be for the characters in *A Confederacy of Dunces.*"

Re-reading my notes about Coles' lecture these many years later, I remembered Robert Gottlieb's dismissive comments about *Confederacy*. "It isn't *really* about anything . . . We could never say that it was anything." In what was subsequently a brilliant career, it was one wrong call, and one he must regret.

Robert Cole was hardly the first to find abundant meaning in the book, and far from the last. Its meaning and significance are being examined, debated, and discussed in college and university classrooms both in the United States and abroad. Graduate students are mining it for theses and dissertations. "The book could be improved and published. But it wouldn't succeed," Gottlieb wrote Ken, but by the time of the Coles lecture the book had sold more than half a million copies and been translated into half a dozen languages. Today it has sold at least a million more copies and achieved the status of a classic.

The reception at the French House on the campus after the lecture was festive with Thelma and Walker Percy receiving as much attention as Dr. Coles. I noticed that the head of the USL English department, Dr. Fields, was there, and there were no obvious firemen. Someone at the reception had the temerity to ask Thelma if Ignatius were like her son.

Her eyebrows went up. "My son like Ignatius? My elegant dresser? My fastidious man who used men's colognes? I used to buy him Aramis! He used to buy and wear very expensive clothes! My son was nothing, nothing like Ignatius!" She stared with contempt at her questioner who did not attempt a second question.

Thelma stayed overnight at a local hotel, and then spent much of Saturday morning visiting with my mother and me. Maurice had arranged for her to be driven back to New Orleans, but he kept calling to say that he and her ride had been delayed.

I asked her what she thought of Coles' interpreting Ignatius as a metaphor for the Roman Catholic Church. "I'll have to think about that," she said. And after she had thought about it for a few seconds, concurred. "He would be," she said. "Ignatius is a booby and a prophet . . . a strange paradox. I'll have to think that over more deeply."

Maurice finally arrived with a couple from New Orleans, Thelma's neighbors who were to give her a ride home.

Almost two years later, after the publication by USL of the Robert Coles lecture, to which was appended a brief memoir by Thelma, she returned to Lafayette for a book signing arranged by Maurice at the Acadiana Book Exchange. It was a rather unlikely venue in which to celebrate the appearance of a university publication. The bookstore, in a converted ranch-style house on University Avenue, specialized in Harlequin romances, paperback Western novels, porno magazines, and waterbeds. If Thelma found it strange, she was too polite to say so. A small group of people from the university and a few friends of Maurice showed up. David Dillon, a librarian at the University of New Orleans, had driven Thelma over for the occasion. The owner of the bookstore was a young blond man with very earnest eyes and a USMC button in his lapel.

Thelma's contribution to the booklet was a three-page-long essay entitled "A Mother's Remembrance; I Walk in the World for My Son." It was a fairly succinct account of Ken's life. She did manage to get a dig in at the despised New York publishing house that first rejected *Confederacy*: "By the way," she wrote, "Simon and Schuster has never had a Pulitzer Prize winner!"

The memoir ended: "My darling's Mt. Parnassus brain and multiplicity of talents forced him to endure many obstacles and trials. But he lives on, and the wonder of him still lingers in the world, and will continue to live! From the one who was the vessel which brought him to life, his mother, Thelma Ducoing Toole."

I stood in the short line at the bookstore and Thelma signed my copy of the pamphlet. After the event, Maurice was taking Thelma, Dr. Dillon, and the bookstore owner to lunch at Don's Seafood Hut, and I invited them to come over to my mother's house for coffee after that. They arrived about three o'clock, accompanied by one of the waiters from the restaurant whom Maurice had asked along. My mother and I served them coffee, we watched on TV the book signing, which had been covered by a local station, and then they departed. While we were all saying our good-byes, Thelma grasped the hand of the dealer in used books and waterbeds, gazed deeply into his eyes, and in her grand elocutionary manner intoned, "I'm proud of you and your bookstore, darling. Keep literature afloat!" she shouted after him as he drove off with Maurice and the waiter.

CHAPTER TWELVE

Thelma and Michael

In September of 1981, Thelma asked me to come to New Orleans to help her entertain a young Hollywood producer and decide whether or not to accept his proposal to make a television movie about the events that led up to the publication of *Confederacy.* From our phone conversations I could tell that she was taken with the idea and charmed by the producer. She told me that according to the terms of the contract, if the movie were actually made, she would receive fifteen thousand dollars. "Quite a hunk of payola!" she remarked.

The producer had arrived in New Orleans the day before I did, and had already been by to see Thelma. She told me that he had arrived fifteen minutes early for their appointment and she had seen him pacing up and down the sidewalk outside the house before he rang the bell. "I was still eating a cheese sandwich and I was very annoyed at first. Then I saw how good-looking he was, and I said to myself, 'Could that be him? Could I really get this lucky?'"

The plan was for me to pick up the producer at the Hilton, deliver him to Thelma's, and then we would all go to lunch. His name was Michael, and he was a partner in the company that hoped to produce the movie.

Michael was waiting for me in the lobby of the Hilton. He was an exceedingly handsome young man in his late twenties, with beautiful brown hair and beautiful brown eyes, one of which was slightly out of focus. He was well tanned and wearing a pink Lacoste knit shirt.

In the car driving over to Elysian Fields, Michael told me something about himself and his production company. His partner did most of the writing, and Michael did most of the marketing. His partner had written the screenplay for at least one very successful movie, and he mentioned several projects they had been involved in together.

"We really don't expect to make money with Thelma's story," he told me, "but we want to do it because it is such a wonderful story. You know, Thelma is very lucky to be dealing with me and Seth. You wouldn't believe how many dishonest people, how many con men there are in Hollywood! She's really very lucky that we are the ones who want to do the story, even though we probably won't make any money out of it at all! It's just the kind of story that needs to be made!"

Thelma, dressed for an occasion, was waiting for us at the door. She had decided that the Maple Hill Restaurant would be a suitable venue for lunch.

Over lunch Michael immediately began to discuss what he wanted to do with the movie. "To make a good movie, we need an interesting hook," he said. "I've been giving this a lot of thought and I would like to run a few things by you. Nothing's settled yet, but I'd like for you to hear some of my thoughts."

"Please do proceed," said Thelma, fixing him with a slightly wary look.

"Now, Thelma, let's just suppose that when Ken was in Puerto Rico he wanted to come back to New Orleans to help you celebrate your sixty-fifth birthday, but he didn't have enough money to buy a ticket. So he takes a part-time job to make the money to pay for the ticket. There you are sitting in your living room feeling very blue because Ken is not with you when suddenly there is a knock at the door. You open it and there is Ken. 'Gee, Mom,' he tells you. 'I knew you really wanted me to be here so I took a part-time job so I could make enough money to be here to celebrate with you.'"

Thelma stared at Michael in disbelief and said nothing.

"Of course, we haven't set anything in stone yet and that is just one idea. I'd like to tell you about some others, too."

Thelma munched on her oyster loaf and sipped her glass of beer and listened to Michael spin a few more bizarre scenarios. When we had finished eating, she said, "I think it is time for me to go and rest now. I don't want to be tired out for John Geiser's dinner party this evening. He's going to a great deal of trouble to entertain us."

Michael had set his camera and light meter on the table. "I'd like to take some photographs of you and Thelma," he said, knocking the light meter to the floor where the batteries flew out. He scrambled to pick them up and tried to cram them back, forcing them in, forcing the top to close. They popped out again. He tried once again to cram them in. Once again they popped out. "I think there's a diagram showing you how the batteries fit in," I offered. He ignored my advice and kept cramming and the batteries kept popping.

Finally he got the batteries back in and the top back on the light meter, probably through sheer luck. Thelma and I posed for a couple of photos in front of the Maple Hill. I wondered how they would come out.

That evening John Geiser, who had been a childhood friend of Ken's, had invited us to dinner at his Garden District home to celebrate Thelma's birthday. He had also invited Douglas Crawford and David Swoyer, close friends of mine who had become friends of Thelma, and we understood that we were all to serve as a kind of unofficial committee to help Thelma make up her mind whether or not to sign the contract. I was to pick up Thelma at a quarter of seven, we were then to pick up Michael at the Hilton at seven, in plenty of time to arrive punctually at John Geiser's where we were invited for seven-thirty. Thelma and I pulled up in front of the Hilton precisely at seven. Michael was not waiting in the appointed spot. At about seven-fifteen he emerged from the hotel with an attractive girl who looked slightly disheveled.

"My goodness," Michael said. "I'm sorry I was late. I was waiting for you on the wrong side of the hotel! I'd like you to meet a friend of mine who I just happened to run into in the hotel. Her fiancé is a dentist and they're here attending a dental convention. She's read Ken's book and wanted to meet you!"

Thelma raised both eyebrows and extended her hand. "Very pleased to meet any fan of my son's book," she said. The girl took Thelma's hand, mumbled something and disappeared back into the Hilton. Michael climbed into the back seat of the car.

"That hotel is really a madhouse," Michael said. "It's filled with drunks and you hear and see some of the most ridiculous things there."

"How disgusting," said Thelma. "You should avoid places like that."

Soon we were seated at John's well-appointed table in his formal dining room. We were supposed to be assessing Michael; but as usual Thelma dominated the conversation and Michael had little chance to produce any evidence for us to build a case for or against him.

After the dinner party, and after we had taken Thelma back home, I asked Michael if he would like to stop for a coffee at that venerable New Orleans institution, Morning Call.

"Why don't you just come back with me to the hotel and we can have a quick drink there?" he suggested.

As we were getting out of the car at the Hilton, Michael said, "Oh, by the way, that girl I introduced you and Thelma to this evening. The story about her fiancé being a dentist and all, and they're being at the hotel, that wasn't true. She's a girl I date when I'm in the South. But I didn't want Thelma to know that I had an attachment to a woman here in New Orleans. I thought she probably wouldn't like it. And I wouldn't have dreamed of taking her to the party. I just didn't think it was a good idea. I'm telling you this because I know it doesn't make any difference to you."

Over drinks in the downtown bar of the Hilton, Michael told me how much he had enjoyed John Geiser's dinner party. "You have such nice friends," he said. I agreed.

"Was Ken gay?" he asked.

His question caught me a little off guard. "I really don't know," I said. "We certainly never discussed it and I always had the impression that Ken was rather asexual. But I've thought that about people before and have been wrong."

"You know," continued Michael, "if we make this movie we are going to have to show a side of Ken that Thelma didn't know. One's mother always sees a person who is not a complete person. That's true of everybody, and we are going to have to show another side of Ken."

Michael had trouble all day absorbing the chronology of Ken's life, and kept getting it mixed up, asking questions that showed he had not listened to what he had been told a few minutes before. As we sat in the bar he made one more attempt to get it all straight, and asked me to help him as he jotted down the basic facts and approximate dates of Ken's life on a paper napkin. We finished our drinks and as I took my leave he was still studying the scribbled notes.

Driving back to David and Douglas's shotgun house uptown, where I was spending the night, I wondered if Thelma was still considering signing the contract. According to her plan, we were to spend the next day with Michael discussing it further.

When I arrived at Thelma's the next morning, I asked her what she had decided to do about the contract.

"I am a little leery of a few things, honey," she said.

"As well I think you might be," I replied.

"Darling," she said, "last night's festivities have left me very weary and I really feel I must rest today. I would greatly appreciate it if you would take Michael to lunch."

So I took Michael to lunch. We drove past Irene's Zoo

Revue Lounge on Camp Street, down shady Esplanade Avenue to Faubourg, a fashionable but not wildly expensive restaurant just outside the Vieux Carré. Today Michael was wearing a red Lacoste shirt. I ordered a chef's salad and he ordered a platter of crab's legs and while we were consuming them and drinking a couple of beers, he told me a lot about himself. He was born in Ohio, he said, but moved to Philadelphia when he was seven. He told me that he went to Brown for a couple of years and studied political science and economics, then got into marketing. He met some guys who were working in the movies, and he realized that they were having a good time, making money, having dates, sleeping late." So Michael went to Hollywood.

After this thumbnail autobiography, Michael returned to the subject of Ken. "So you think Ken might have been bisexual?"

"Actually, asexual is what I said. He never struck me as being particularly interested in sex," I told him once again. "Somehow he gave me the impression that he was above all that. But I might have been wrong. I probably was. "

"I've known people like that," said Michael. "In fact, I have a good friend in Los Angeles, a producer, works at Paramount. He is forty-four and unmarried. He's the same way. We go to Vegas together a couple of times a year. He works on the series *Vegas* so they always give him this big suite free, and it only has one bed in it, and we take it because it's free, and I always sleep with him, we share the same bed. He never makes advances at me. It doesn't bother me. But my partner and a lot of other people in Hollywood think I've been sleeping with Gary!"

"Isn't that what you just told me?" I asked. He was lost in his thoughts and didn't seem to get it.

"I don't know why straight men . . . most straight men feel so insecure with homosexuals," he continued. "I certainly don't," he said. "I have some good friends in Los Angeles who are homosexuals, and I feel very comfortable with them. "He leaned over and said in a more confidential tone, "In fact, for part of my life I *was* a homosexual!"

"For which part?" I asked.

"For two years, from twelve to fourteen. With my friend Benny. He was sixteen. I came out of it about fourteen, and you know it gave me such a guilt complex that I stayed a virgin, with girls, that is, until I was almost nineteen."

"Well, nineteen is not so bad, except maybe in the South!"

"Listen," he said, "here's an idea that's right off the wall." (Which of his ideas hadn't been?) "Now what if Ken had met Gottlieb while he was still in New York, you know, like, when he was still at Columbia, like before he wrote the book, and what if he got involved with him, and then, and then, Gottlieb rejected him. That would at least explain why Ken didn't want to send the manuscript to anywhere but Simon and Schuster, wouldn't it?"

"Would it?" This was the wildest of Michael's wild ideas. I fervently hoped that Thelma would never sign the contract.

After lunch, it was time for me to head back to Lafayette. Michael planned to spend another couple of days in New Orleans. Thelma would have to cope with him on her own. But by then I was fairly sure that Michael would return to

California with his contract for the television movie unsigned.

Next day, Michael telephoned from New Orleans. He had decided to come to Lafayette to talk to Pat and Milton Rickels, who had been amongst Ken's closest friends there. He had also telephoned Bobby Byrne, but had been rebuffed. Michael reported their brief conversation verbatim: "I'm about to burn a steak," Bobby told him, "and I really do not think this conversation is worth any further char. If you are calling to ask whether Ken Toole and I were bosom buddies, the answer in a word is no."

I don't recall if Michael made it to Lafayette or not. I don't know whether he interviewed the Rickels or not. Thelma did not sign the contract. Thelma mentioned later that Michael had tried to buy the rights to a long, two-part article about Ken by New Orleans writer Dalt Wonk, which appeared in the Sunday magazine of the *Times-Picayune* in November of 1981.

But in any case, the movie was never made. And probably a very good thing that it wasn't.

Many years have passed since Thelma summoned me to New Orleans to help her cope with and pass judgment on Michael. Re-reading the journals I kept and the tape recordings I made then, the episode comes clearly back to mind, and I can see in my mind's eye Michael in his Lacoste knit shirts, handsome, seductive, charming, confused, bumbling, and ingenuous with his wild plot ideas.

I do a Google search and find a Michael of the same last name in Hollywood, the president of a major studio. Could it possibly be? Did the Michael I met have executive potential that I somehow missed? But then I notice that the studio president is "Michael G." not "Michael J." I scroll down the screen and find a "Michael J." also in Hollywood. He is listed as one of the writers of a 1989 Tony Danza movie. A review gives the movie one star and a half, calls the screenplay "superficial" and the movie "silly and contrived." Yes, that must be Michael.

CHAPTER THIRTEEN

Lunches with the Percys

A few weeks after the Robert Coles lecture in Lafayette, Thelma called to tell me that we were invited to have lunch with Walker and Bunt Percy at their home in Covington, and asked me to telephone him for directions. "He can be irascible," she warned me, "So be careful what you say." When I called he was anything but irascible. He was very cordial and very Southern-gentle, and gave me clear directions to their new house on the banks of Tchefuncta River.

I picked up Thelma at Elysian Fields on a Friday morning in early October. The weather was almost cool. The sky was cloud-less and the causeway across Lake Pontchartrain was traffic-less as we zipped over to Covington. Following the directions, we easily found the house, an Acadian-style cottage with a tin roof at the end of a tree-lined gravel road.

Walker, dressed in a flannel shirt, cotton trousers, and blue running shoes, came out to greet us when we pulled up in front of the house. Bunt was waiting at the door, a pleasant-looking woman wearing glasses, simply dressed in a skirt and blouse. They showed us into a house that seemed barely lived in. The bookcases that lined the central hall were only sparsely filled with books, and everything looked shiny-new. The floors were of pretty, well-polished tile, with a few handsome oriental rugs. A large back room, a kind of sitting room/dining room, had a wall of tall windows looking out toward the river, which was almost invisible beyond a screen of trees. Most of the furniture in this handsome room was metal porch furniture with bright cushions, obviously a make-do arrangement until proper furniture arrived. In its midst was a noble Italian refectory table that lent a distinguished air.

The Percys's daughter, Ann, born deaf, joined us in a little while. By lip reading she took part in the conversation, and she spoke of her son, who was also born deaf. I liked her quiet and easy manner.

A few minutes later, Will Percy, Walker's nephew, arrived. He was blond, good-looking, small, animated, polite, and very charming. Will, Walker told us, had just graduated from law school and begun to practice law in Covington.

We sat in the pretty back room on the temporary furniture. Thelma had a glass of wine. Walker and I sipped bourbon. When Thelma mildly upbraided Walker for having inaccurately described what she was wearing when they first met, he replied: "Yes, it's true. I'm not very observant. You would think that being a novelist I would remember things that I see, but I don't. Bunt is much better at that than I am. She doesn't miss anything"

We moved to the table and Thelma, as usual, dominated the conversation, warming to an audience that appreciated her.

When Walker got a word in, it was to mention that he had heard that a female scholar at a Mid-western university had written an article proving to her own satisfaction that *Confederacy* was a literary hoax, that Ken Toole had never existed, and that it was really written by Walker with Thelma's help.

On the way back to New Orleans, Thelma told me how much she had enjoyed the day. It had been, she said, the first time she had had a chance to sit down and really talk with Walker. She had done most of the talking, of course, but he didn't seem to mind, and much of what she said reflected her unflawed gratitude to him. That day she looked as happy as I had ever seen her.

About six weeks later, in early December, my mother and I hosted a luncheon party at my mother's home in Lafayette. Walker and Bunt drove over from Covington and Thelma was chauffeured from New Orleans by her neighbors on Elysian Fields. I also invited a couple from the history department at USL, who were very old friends of mine, and the eccentric lawyer who handled the Flora Levy estate.

My mother was a few years older than Thelma, and had been widowed for a decade when this party took place. I lived across the driveway from my mother's house in a little cottage that my parents had given me. I was near enough, but not too near. We both valued our independence. But we saw a lot of each other and had many of our meals together. My mother was very good company, had a dry wit, and a way with words. After a two-day visit from a friend of mine, whom my mother found tiresome, I overheard her telling someone: "Joel's friend, S., spent a month with us last weekend." A year later, a stroke would change her radically, but on the day of our party for Thelma and the Percys, her only problem was deafness, which was growing more difficult for her to deal with. She had a hearing aid, but complained that the amplification let her hear too much, and much of it just noise.

Thelma arrived in emerald green with white gloves. Confronted with a room of people, some she had never seen before, she inevitably went "on stage." Without requesting it, we were treated to a series of her "interpretations" of characters from *Confederacy*. She finished to applause and compliments of varying degrees of sincerity. And then we ate.

I had fixed lunch. My mother, like a number of Southern women of her generation and station in life, took a certain amount of pride in her reputation as a terrible cook. It was a way of letting the world know that she had never had to do domestic chores. During her many years as a college president's wife, she had acquired a well-deserved reputation as a gracious hostess, but being a gracious hostess did not include doing the cooking and the washing up. She was very happy that her bachelor son had learned various culinary skills in his years abroad and on his own.

The main course that day was a huge shrimp salad, served with a decent *frascati* and hot potato rolls. The *zuppa inglese* I had prepared for dessert seemed to be a big hit. And then we had little Wedgwood demitasses of hot, black coffee, a tradition in southern Louisiana. Bunt helped me carry the empty plates back into the kitchen, and when we were alone, she smiled and said, "Your mother is just a little bit jealous of Thelma, isn't she. I picked up on that." I had not noticed what Bunt had, that halfway through Thelma's recitations, Mother had quietly removed her hearing aid.

I had noticed that in the middle of one of Thelma's "interpretations," Mother, in her deafness not realizing a performance was still going on at her right elbow, began telling a story to Bunt in a loud voice. Thelma stopped and smiled at her indulgently. Such an impertinence committed by anyone else would have received a withering stare and an acid remark. But the two women were always very kind to each other. I noted in my journal: "Thelma sends Mother little gifts: scarves, costume jewelry, chocolates, and Mother writes her charming little thank-you notes." Six months before her death, Thelma wrote my mother a note which began: "Dear Miss Fannie, If we were neighbors, what brisk, bright conversations we would enjoy! That 'ole dibbel' distance frustrates us." Mother was fond of Thelma, but was no doubt grateful for the distance that kept her visits from being too frequent. She was perhaps a little jealous, but that did not interfere with her enjoyment of life and her appreciation of Thelma.

A few days after the party, we had a thank-you note from Bunt. She had sent with it, for my mother, a thoughtful gift, a kind of tape that made wearing a hearing aid more comfortable, something she had discovered in her years of dealing with much more serious problems of deafness in her own family.

Chapter Fourteen

Thelma vs. Rhoda Faust, Thelma vs. the Tooles, and Other Feuds

Walker Percy, after he had read the manuscript of *Confederacy,* and while he was looking for someone to publish it, gave it to his friend, Rhoda Faust, owner of the Maple Street Book Shop. Faust loved the book and was one of the first to befriend Thelma because of it. In a *Times-Picayune* article about the coming publication of the book, she was quoted as saying that it was "profound, rich, and hilariously funny throughout," an opinion that would be echoed by many critics after the book appeared. She was also quoted in the same story as saying that she was going to publish Ken's first novel, *The Neon Bible*, written when he was sixteen. Her intention to do so became a major cause of the ugly quarrel between Thelma and Faust.

Ken wrote *The Neon Bible*, a novella inspired by a brief trip to rural Mississippi with his high school classmate Cary Laird, for a literary contest. The story, strongly influenced by the dark tales of Flannery O'Connor, one of his idols, did not win the contest. Ken never again tried to have it published, just as after the rejection of *Confederacy* by Simon and Schuster he quickly gave up on the novel that would win him posthumous fame.

In the spring of 1979, Faust gave a party at her bookstore near Tulane to celebrate the forthcoming publication of *Confederacy*. It is a very literary bookstore, housed in a typical New Orleans shotgun-style house on a narrow, tree-shaded street. The shelves are filled with books that reflect Ms. Faust's interesting and idiosyncratic tastes. Many Southern authors and books about New Orleans can be found here, as well as selections from the *New York Times* list of best-sellers and relatively obscure books one would not easily find in a chain bookstore. The back room is large enough to accommodate an audience for literary readings and receptions. Where there are no shelves, the walls are covered with newspaper clippings about books and writers and with photographs of the blonde, wiry, tough-looking Ms. Faust posing with famous authors.

The friendship between the two women did not last long. A year after the party Faust gave in her honor, Thelma and Rhoda were no longer speaking but were instead exchanging angry letters, Thelma's written by her lawyers.

While they were still on good terms, Thelma had lent Faust the manuscript of *The Neon Bible*, the original correspondence between Ken and Simon and Schuster, a number of scrapbooks with photographs of Ken, and his school papers. Before she had begun to receive royalties from LSU Press, Thelma was, as usual, short of money, and she had also consigned a number of books from Ken's library for sale at the bookstore, including Ken's set of *Harvard Classics.*

Faust has been quoted as saying that she had wanted to publish *Confederacy*, and had received Thelma's blessing to do so, but that she had not at the time been able to come up with the money needed. Then Thelma had given her a copy of *The Neon Bible* and promised her that she could publish it, eventually. Thelma, Faust said, wanted to delay publication of the earlier novel until people had been given sufficient time "to meditate on the glory of *Confederacy*." Faust claims that Thelma told her several times that when she was ready to let it be published, Faust would be the one to publish *The Neon Bible*. But she never gave her this permission in writing.

After the friendship between the two women ended in 1980, Thelma did get back from Faust the manuscript of *The Neon Bible* and the scrapbooks, but she was never again to see the originals of the correspondence between Ken and Simon and Schuster. Rhoda told her that an employee who had been sent to the post office to mail the letters back to Thelma, had accidentally dropped the envelope containing them in the street, and, though she had gone back to look for them, she had been unable to find them. Fortunately, photocopies of the correspondence had been made and a number of copies of them still exist.

When the relationship between Thelma and Faust soured, Thelma still intended to let *The Neon Bible* be published, but she came upon what in her mind was an insurmountable problem.

Both Ken and his father had died without a will, and under Louisiana law, which is based on the Napoleonic Code, 50 percent of the publication rights to both *Confederacy* and *The Neon Bible* belonged to the heirs of Ken's paternal uncle, who, according to bizarre Louisiana law, was the heir of Thelma's husband. Thelma had managed to get the heirs—three nieces and a nephew—to sign waivers relinquishing all claims to *Confederacy* before it was published. But when they realized that *Confederacy* was a great success, they refused to sign similar waivers with regard to *The Neon Bible*. Fueled by her contempt and dislike of her husband's family, waging battle with them became a sad obsession in Thelma's last years. When the heirs failed to show up at a meeting arranged by Thelma's lawyer to sign off on *The Neon Bible*, in a rage, she wrote them an emotional, denunciatory, threatening letter. In part, it read:

> In the eyes of God and the eyes of man, "The Neon Bible" is the exclusive and righteous property of the creator, John Kennedy Toole . . . My husband, your uncle, made an enviable record at Warren Easton High School as a mathematical wizard and a Champion State Debater in a rally at LSU, in Baton Rouge, La. By some quirk of mind, he chose to be an automobile salesman; no standing in the community and no decent income, causing great distress over forty-five years of marriage.
>
> I supported our marriage, and I nurtured my literary and scholarly genius by my superior teaching ability and high degree of culture.
>
> At the present time, I am in contact with someone of rare legal ability, seeking to have the outrageous law repealed.
>
> If I am not successful, "The Neon Bible" will not be published, and a terrible blight will fall upon those responsible for this nefarious act.

Thelma also wrote a letter to the governor of Louisiana, David Treen, asking for his intervention:

My husband's four relatives are ordinary working people, with no sound education, no vestige of culture, and interminable quarreling in their family circles. They are basically and truly unfit to represent my son, and share the fruits of his highly-gifted creative ability.

I have formed "A Coalition for the Advocacy of Protecting The Neon Bible from Unjust Claimants" by contacting several attorneys and one judge to whom I taught Speech and Dramatic Art years ago. They are giving consideration to the matter.

Thelma's efforts were, of course, all in vain, and her "Coalition" was no more effective than Ignatius's absurd "Crusade for Moorish Dignity" in *Confederacy*. Finally Thelma decided that she would rather try to prevent the publication of *The Neon Bible* than let the Toole relatives have any share of its potential profit. She held her brilliant, ineffectual husband responsible for all the woes in her life, and, by extension, his family.

In her will, Thelma left her half interest in *The Neon Bible* to her friend, University of New Orleans professor Kenneth Holditch, on the condition that it was never to be published. Holditch respected her wishes and as a result found himself embroiled in lawsuits filed by the Toole heirs and Rhoda Faust.

The week before Thelma died, Rhoda Faust filed a suit to force her to honor what Faust still claimed was her promise to let her publish the book. Eventually, a civil district judge in New Orleans ruled that Faust's claim to an oral contract with Thelma was not valid.

The same judge later ruled that Thelma had no right to

leave *The Neon Bible* to Holditch because she only owned part of it, and that if Holditch and the Toole heirs could not agree on its publication, the book, just like a piece of jointly-owned real estate, should be sold at public auction. Faced with this decision, Holditch capitulated. To avoid the public auction, he and the heirs sold the rights to the book to Grove Press, which had brought out the first paperback edition of *Confederacy*, and it was published by them in 1989.

The Neon Bible did not have the enormous success of *Confederacy*, but it received a number of favorable reviews. Michiko Kakutani, writing in the *New York Times,* liked it better than *Confederacy*. "*The Neon Bible*," she wrote, "emerges as an altogether more organic and satisfying novel—a novel that works on the reader not through willful manipulation, but through heartfelt emotion, communicated in clean, direct prose." She concludes by saying that the novel " . . . not only stands as a remarkable achievement for a 16-year-old writer, but it also serves as a testament (more valid than "Dunces" in this critic's opinion) to the genuine talents of Toole."

In 1996, the English director Terence Davies made a movie of *The Neon Bible* starring Gena Rowlands as the flamboyant Aunt Mae. Readers of *Confederacy* have often assumed that the character of Irene Reilly was based on Thelma, but there is much more of Thelma in the frustrated singer Aunt Mae than in the vulgar and uneducated Irene. The film also received some favorable reviews in the press, but was never given a wide distribution.

It is ironic that *The Neon Bible*, generally viewed more as a curiosity than a valid work of art, became a movie so shortly after it was published, while *Confederacy*, about which there has swirled so much interest since its publication, has not yet made it to the screen. Hollywood producer Scott Kramer bought the movie rights in 1980 for $10,000, and for a short time, it seemed as if the production of the movie was imminent. Thelma, of course, had very strong ideas about how the movie should be made, and wanted total control over it. She was furious when she found out through Walker Percy that LSU Press had signed a contract with Kramer without her knowledge, but accepted the fact that Kramer had acquired the rights. She sent me a copy of the letter she wrote him:

> The writer, Thelma Ducoing Toole, mother of the brilliant novelist, John Kennedy Toole, has had a keen urge to communicate with you about the forthcoming movie, "Confederacy of Dunces."
>
> This is based upon sixteen years of Dramatic Art Training, in which I was successful as a performer, teacher, and director.
>
> When you formulate plans for the movie, will you give me an opportunity to speak with the scenario writer and director? I am hoping to be of substantial assistance to them, because I have insight into the characters about whom my son writes so explicitly and impressively.
>
> May the movie bring mounting financial rewards and noteworthy praise, in return for your astute judgment in securing production rights.
>
> Looking forward! Thelma Ducoing Toole

I don't know how Kramer responded to this letter, but it is unlikely that he shared her enthusiasm for their collaboration. The story of *Confederacy* not being made into a movie could itself be made into a movie or a book. An article by John Lippman in the *Wall Street Journal* (September 30, 1999) charted some of the vicissitudes of the project's history, and mentioned that in the almost twenty years since the rights were first sold, the project has had seven producers, six scripts, and five studios. Several of the actors who were suggested to play Ignatius Reilly—John Belushi, John Candy, and Chris Farley—are now deceased. According to the *Wall Street Journal,* Scott Kramer is still attempting to make the film.

Thelma created other enemies for herself. Even though Les Phillabaum, editor of LSU Press, had been instrumental in getting *Confederacy* published, Thelma soon also turned against him for no good reason. The first inkling I had that things had begun to go wrong between them was when she wrote me in July 1980, shortly after the first edition of *Confederacy* had appeared.

> It is nine days since I have written to Mr. Phillabaum. I feel he is somewhat startled because, I think, he regards me as a passive person. Little does he know how I vibrate, analyze, and pulsate on the inside.

If he didn't know, he was soon to find out. Thelma did not understand the way LSU handled the royalties for the book, and began to suspect they were delaying payment and not being up front with her. I believe the truth of the matter was that she simply would like to have had complete control over the book and resented LSU Press's normal exercise of their rights. Thelma began to write and speak derisively of Phillabaum, and to pester him about her payments. In June of 1981, she wrote me: "I phoned 'Philly-bomb,' and as of today, no check."

Sometime after Thelma had begun to feud seriously with Phillabaum, I met the promotion manager for LSU Press at a party in Baton Rouge. Catherine Silvia vigorously defended her boss. "Les doesn't care at all what people think of him. He has done so many things that have changed people's lives and they never know. He doesn't care if he gets the credit. He has devoted his life to the Press and his son . . . thinks about nothing else." I suggested that he might remedy the situation with Thelma by paying her a little more attention. She told me that the chancellor of LSU had at one time planned a party for Thelma, but that it had never materialized and that Les felt he couldn't push it. "After Grove Press flew Thelma to New York, gave her the royal treatment, he didn't want to play one-upmanship with Grove."

To the end of her life, Thelma never forgave the slights she imagined she had received from one who had done so much to make the publication of *Confederacy* possible.

In January of 1983, I saw an article in the Baton Rouge *Morning Advocate* about a musical version of *Confederacy* being produced by the LSU drama department. I cut it out and sent it to Thelma. She knew nothing about it, and was once again furious with Phillabaum. The following month, Phillabaum did write to Thelma about the musical. He wrote that the well-known director Frank Galati was being brought in to prepare a script and direct, and that Galati and a Dr. Doty of the LSU faculty would be in touch with her about it. Unfortunately, they did not write or phone

Thelma, and just before the production was to open she wrote to them:

> Dr. Doty and Dr. Gallatti [sic]
>
> Your gross negligence, in not consulting me about the forthcoming musical stage play, astounded me! Even though LSU Press has control of movie, stage, and television rights (my contract states so), you should have inherently, legally, logically and righteously acknowledged that "I Am Owner, in Staunch Alliance with the eminent writer, Dr. Walker Percy."
>
> As members of the Groves of Academe, you should maintain high ideals: respect for authority, and a keen evaluation of worth.

On the copy of the letter that Thelma sent me, she had written, "This aptly expresses my resentment."

Once the production opened, all was forgiven, and Thelma made a joyous appearance on opening night. The rave review by David Foil in the Baton Rouge *Advocate* described Thelma's reaction:

> Mrs. Toole was still riding high at the show's conclusion. Stepping out of character, Harlan [the actor who played Ignatius] introduced Mrs. Toole to the audience. Most 82-year-olds would have remained seated, acknowledging the audience's applause with a wave of the hand. Some might have stood briefly. Mrs. Toole stood slowly. Then, she made a speech.
>
> "This has been a beautiful evening in the American theater," Mrs. Toole proclaimed.
>
> She ended her speech with, "May it go to Broadway and run and run and run."

Mrs. Toole sat with long-stemmed red roses in her lap as the audience filed slowly out of the theater.

Thelma's wars with Rhoda Faust, the Toole relatives, and Les Phillabaum, and her struggle to control the making of the movie of Ken's great novel, cast shadows over her triumphant last years. She was a fighter, and she found fights to fight until the end, and, in her eyes, justice was always entirely on her side.

The other great cause for distress in the last years of her life was her deteriorating health.

CHAPTER FIFTEEN

"A Way Out of this Dilemma of Being Alive"

Thelma began having serious health problems in the spring of 1982, and in June of that year went into Baptist Hospital for tests. I visited her there and found her in good spirits. When I arrived she was telling her roommate the story of how she had got *Confederacy* published, and was so engrossed in her tale that she did not notice me for a little while. When she did, she plopped down and pulled the covers over her head in childish delight, peeping out and smiling and being what she would have called "flirtatious." I sat with her for almost two hours and listened to her spirited description of her adventures in the hospital and everything else that was going on in her life. A biopsy of a growth in her kidney was scheduled for later that day.

Back home a few days later, she telephoned to say that the biopsy had gone well, but she had not yet received the results.

The biopsy had not gone well. The growth was cancerous, and Thelma was soon returning to Baptist Hospital for x-ray treatments. In early July she phoned again to say the treatment was "barbarous" and that she had decided not to go for another. "Death is preferable," she said.

She was in a rage. And then she told me that I was not to call her, write her, send her books. After the call I received a letter which had been written a few days before it:

> I am withdrawing my request for your solicitous and personable escort service. Your business and personal interests are manifold, and I don't want to cause any interruption. The long, tedious drive to and from New Orleans, the expenditure of time, the needless expense of overnight lodging, make my decision unselfish, substantial, and considerate. I must cope alone with my health dilemma. I am a solitary person, and I know my physical and nervous systems. My son, the only true friend I ever had, and the only person who truly loved me is not here to solace me. If I regain some measure of health and some degree of composure, I'll contact you. Please don't answer this letter! Earnestly, Thelma.

She was obviously in great distress and lashing out. I ignored her request and wrote a brief note saying how grieved I was over her illness and the fact that I had not been able to see her more often, and that I hoped she would prevail over her present sadness as she had over the other sadnesses in her life.

A few days later I telephoned and found her in better spirits.

"I came into the living room because I knew it was the hour you used to call," she said. And she spoke of her gloom. "My French blood gave me my taste in clothes and literature. My Irish blood gave me my sense of doom. 'Bring me my shroud,' my Irish grandmother used to cackle every time she felt low. I wondered what it looked like, and asked my sister, Margaret. Brown! She told me it was brown!"

By the end of the month, Thelma was feeling much better, and I learned in a phone call from her why she had been angry with me. She felt that when I had been in New Orleans a few months earlier exhibiting at an antiques show, I had not paid her enough attention.

"When you were at the Rivergate you were wining and dining every night and only came to see me once for breakfast. You said you'd be here at 7 and didn't show up until 7:30. You said the alarm didn't go off, and then after you had breakfast you scooted off and I didn't see you again. You should have called me every day!"

She had forgotten that I had come over after the show and spent a whole afternoon driving her around. I realized that she was ill and irrational. A few days later she phoned again. "You're still number one. All is forgiven."

She telephoned a week later after a session of chemotherapy, which she was finding ever more difficult to bear. And she was worried about the expense, probably with no good reason. "I may be looking for some way out of this dilemma of being alive," she said.

But gradually she seemed to get better and resumed her busy social life and her role promoting and defending *Confederacy.*

While Thelma was monitoring the progress of the proposed film of *Confederacy,* and trying very hard to exercise complete control over it, she received several other proposals for projects relating to the novel and the story of its publication. The aborted television movie was only one of a number. She was also approached by several people who wished to write Ken's biography. James Allsup, a professor of English at the University of Texas at San Antonio, was probably the best qualified to do so. He had known Ken in Puerto Rico and was already the author of a well-received critical study of the English poet, Percy Bysshe Shelley. The letter Thelma wrote in response to his query must have quickly extinguished his hopes. She wrote, in part:

> You would have to live in my home for several months, perhaps a year, perhaps more. Then you would have to read carefully a wealth of material pertaining to my son, then you and I would decide what to use, what not to use. Then we would begin a collaboration. In the first place, my brother would not permit this. In the second place, I am under the care of a heart specialist.

Typically, unreasonably, Thelma was not going to relinquish an iota of control.

Following her seeming recovery, there was a gradual cooling of our friendship. She had blown up at me several times when she thought I was not paying her enough attention, but she had always got over these bouts of anger. Then in 1982 my mother had a stroke and looking after her took more and more of my time and energy. I could no longer easily get away to New Orleans to squire Thelma about. In any case, her fame had brought her a host of available escorts and companions, and I realized I was no longer as important in her life as I once had been. I was a little grateful for this development. I was certainly fond of her, but I was beginning to suffer a bit from "Thelma burn-out" and was more than content to start taking a back seat to some of her other favorites.

Thelma had become a full-blown local celebrity and her progress could be charted on the social pages of New Orleans newspapers. In February of 1982 she was named one of the "Sweet Arts" of the Krewe of Clones, the carnival organization of the New Orleans Contemporary Art Center, and rode on a float in their parade with other honorees of the Krewe, including Representative Lindy Boggs, and Sybil Morial, wife of the mayor. The event was given extensive coverage by *The Times-Picayune/States-Item.* The theme of the festivities was *A Confederacy of Dunces,* and many of the Krewe came dressed as characters from the novel.

> Red was the look for all the mavens except Thelma, who chose a gold dress and topped it with a chapeau confection. She also manifested a spirit of largesse, distributing gifts to choice chums. They were striped pillowcases in Maison Blanche bags, which went to one gent with the admonition, "No pillow talk, my dear."

That her list of favorites had grown was evidenced by a ceremony to which she invited me on the last day of February of 1982. Ten of her "escorts" were summoned to 1016 Elysian Fields for "investiture" as knights of "Thelma's Imperial Realm." Nine of us appeared. In addition to myself there were: Adolfo Saracho, the Consul General of Argentina, who had hosted and hoisted Thelma aboard the *Punta Norte;* Douglas Crawford, the teacher at

Jesuit High School on whom Thelma had come to rely for all sorts of errands; Russell Rocke, owner of the Toulouse Street Theater; Randy Powell, the owner of the Fleur de Paris hat shop in the French Quarter, who had recently held a soiree in his shop for Thelma; John Geiser, one of Ken's boyhood friends; a Mr. Durham, the husband of one of Thelma's former students; and Philip Yeager, the president of Southeastern University in New Orleans, which had presented Thelma with an honorary degree. (Some months after the ceremony, Southeastern University was exposed in the press as a "diploma mill" and shortly thereafter ceased to exist.)

For the "investiture," Thelma was wearing her Clones outfit of gold silk and the white straw and marabou hat that the society columnist of the *Times-Picayune* had described as "a chapeau confection." We knelt before her and she tapped each one of us on our right shoulders with a rod covered in gold sequins and topped with a miniature French horn. "In the name of Education, Letters, Art, Music, Beauty, and Justice," she proclaimed, and presented each of us with a sterling silver heart-shaped bookmark.

The last letter I have from Thelma is dated December 5, 1983. In it she tells me about a reception planned for her by a Lieutenant Colonel Munger and his wife. She wrote that John Geiser and David Dillon would be providing the transportation. "If you can spare the time, I would warmly welcome you to join us." For whatever reason, I wasn't able to join them, and probably another black mark against me appeared in Thelma's book.

In the same letter she wrote: "I am so beset by ill-health

and worries that my vision is dimming."

In July of 1984, her physical condition worsened. I wrote in my journal:

> I am getting up early tomorrow to drive to New Orleans. I have been summoned by Thelma, in her gloomiest Irish voice, from another one of her death beds. It may well be that when I get there she will have once again miraculously recovered and be preparing for some august social occasion, ready to go forth bearing the light for Ken. But somehow I feel that now she is getting near the end. 'Come,' she said, 'and let us talk of the happy times we had.' And we did have some.

The next day I woke long before dawn, and was in New Orleans by 7:30 A.M. I wrote in my journal:

> Breakfast and the *Times-Picayune* at La Péniche, then went to Schwegmann's to buy fresh fruit and frozen strawberries for Thelma. I had also bought some Fabergé bath powder for her before leaving Lafayette. At 1016 Elysian Fields I found only Arthur, his concave chest was shirtless, but at least his trousers were zipped up. He told me that Thelma was in the intensive care unit of the St. Charles Hospital. Poor Arthur, who is so abused by her, looked genuinely upset. I left the fruit with him and drove to the hospital. I found Thelma on the fourth floor, lying on her bed looking as if she had fallen there from a great height, sprawled, asleep. I touched her brow, kissed it. She opened her eyes and said in a clear voice: 'Who do you represent?'
> 'It's Joel, Thelma.'

'Oh, honey. I've thought so much about you. That's all that's kept me going.' I talked, as she asked me to, about our good times in New York, about Tom Snyder, Anthony Quinn, Toronto, driving around New Orleans, City Park, Lake Pontchartrain, eating fried oysters. She smiled. I mentioned the premiere of the movie and reminded her that I would be one of her escorts. We talked about it and what we would wear to it. It made her happy to fantasize about this future event which grows less likely all the time. I stayed with her for about half an hour, then an aide came to give her a bath. 'Go home now, honey,' she directed as she always did. 'Go home. I love you.' 'I love you, too, Thelma.'

It seems unlikely that I will ever see her alive again. The tumor in her kidney requires her to undergo dialysis, but she refuses to take it.

On August 10, an eccentric lawyer friend, who was usually up before the crack of dawn, called me at 6:45 A.M. to tell me that the *Times-Picayune* had a story about Rhoda Faust suing Thelma to make her keep her promise to let her publish *The Neon Bible.* Thelma died one week later.

It was pouring with rain when I left Lafayette, again early in the morning, to drive to Thelma's funeral in New Orleans, and the weather was a mess for most of the way. I was held up for half an hour by a nine-car accident on the lake bridge just outside of New Orleans. As usual, I had breakfast at La Péniche, then went to the funeral home. By then the sun was out. It stayed out all day, the city cooled by the rain. It almost felt like a fall day. Very unusual for New Orleans in August.

Thelma was dressed in one of her pink gowns, chosen by

Douglas, her white-gloved hands holding a corsage, lying in a dark wooden coffin in the second-floor parlor of Schoen's Funeral Home, the Elysian Fields branch, just down the street from the house she shared with Arthur. The same funeral home had handled the arrangements for Ken's funeral fifteen years before.

Arthur looked devastated and forlorn, swallowed up in a dark blue suit that he wore with a dark shirt, dark tie, and dark blue running shoes. He was sitting in an armchair next to the casket, alone in the parlor. Poor Arthur, who did so much for Thelma, took her in and gave her a place to live when she was in the nursing home after her husband's death, and ran all her errands, went to see her daily when she was in the hospital, and was always so abused and reviled by her ("My brudder! Have you ever seen such a sight! A throwback . . . to what I've never been able to figure out!") They had had blistering rows for years and he was utterly devoted to her. "I've nothing else to live for," he kept saying during the wake.

Thelma's former student Miriam Neeb, also abused by Thelma of late, and Douglas were sitting in the adjoining foyer. After I had talked for a while with Arthur, and tried to say something that would comfort him, and after I had gone up to pay my respects to Thelma, Douglas and Miriam and I were shown to a room with a coffee urn by a woman who kept calling us "dah-lins." Sitting around a Formica-topped table, we helped ourselves to sugar and powdered dairy substitute, which was contained in a most unfuneral, gaily colored ceramic bowl with a smiling cow on its cover.

Miriam told us about her persistent, but unsuccessful,

attempts to get Thelma back into the Catholic Church. "Ah used to call her aw'most every day! But she wouldn't listen to nothin Ah had to tell'er!" "Now, Ah'm so wu-wed about Aw-thur. He looks so ee-man-ci-pated!"

"Yes," said Douglas, always the high school teacher, "he does look *e-mac-i-ated* today." He did justice, as Thelma would have done, to every syllable of the correction.

There was some confusion as to who would serve as pall-bearers. Douglas, who had been doing most of the funeral arrangements, had not yet got around to deciding, or to asking Arthur. As time for the service approached, Arthur began to worry about whether there would be enough men around. "I guess ya need six," he said.

"Don't worry," said Douglas, there are plenty of people around. Anyway, it's no big deal. All you have to do is pick up the casket!"

After some conversation, Douglas, John Geiser, Robbie Kirn (the son of one of Thelma's former students), a man who may have been a pilot (he had a silver airplane pin in his buttonhole), and I were more-or-less designated pall-bearers. Then a pushy woman in green who no one seemed to know arrived and took over. From his demeanor toward her, Arthur seemed to think she was important. John Geiser was bumped and the husband of the woman in green, an elderly, but distinguished-looking and handsome man, replaced him. The woman in green also took over Arthur, held on to him, hovered over him throughout the wake and the service. "Just the kind of woman Thelma would have hated," John Geiser whispered to me.

Walker and Bunt Percy arrived and we had a cordial

chat, remembering Thelma and the several happy occasions we had spent together. Walker asked to be introduced to Arthur, whom he had never met. I took him and Bunt over, and then it was time to move to the chapel downstairs for the Mass.

The priest who presided looked as if he had been found at Schwegmann's. He was doddering and had a strong Irish Channel accent: "In de name ob de fadder, an de son, an de holy spirit." He seemed not terribly far from his own funeral Mass, and read the service perfunctorily and with difficulty, stumbling over words, getting lost in the text. How Thelma would have dealt with his sloppy enunciation! He was never quite erect, but leaned either forward or backward. His hair was a dead-looking gray and his face a chalky-white; his eyebrows still inky black, like two anchovies unrolled on his forehead.

From Schoen's, the funeral procession drove up Elysian Fields, turned to get on Esplanade, and finally arrived at the Greenwood Cemetery at the foot of Canal Street. At the graveside, the Irish Channel priest sprinkled holy water on the casket, and said that Thelma was anointed "by de earl of Salvation." Thelma would have loved that! She could have done him to a T.

Thelma was laid to rest in the tomb with her Ken. John, the disappointing husband, is buried elsewhere, I assume among his own kinfolk, for whom Thelma had such contempt. "Unworthy people, hairdressers and the like . . . the kind of people who buy second-hand Cadillacs," as she frequently described them. Now she was safely away from the Toole relatives she despised, safely away from Rhoda Faust and the other people who bedeviled her, away as well from the people she bedeviled, and also away from those who were fond of her and admired her, were inspired by her courage and remarkable persistence. She and her beloved Ken were together for eternity.

Postscript

Sometime after the death of Thelma in 1984, I retrieved a suitcase of papers that I had left behind in Florence when I moved to Paris in 1967. It contained, among many other letters, the ones that Ken had written to me between 1962 and 1965, and letters from Nicholas Polites and J. C. Broussard that mentioned Ken. Re-reading them, I decided that I should write down what I knew of Ken, drawing from both the letters and from a journal I had kept in the early 1960s. The result was an essay which I sent around to various magazines, including, optimistically, the *New Yorker, Harper's,* the *Atlantic Monthly,* and the *New York Review of Books.* Each time the essay came back with a rejection slip. I finally put it aside, thinking that perhaps I would pick it up one day and add to it the information I had about Thelma. It eventually became, with much alteration, the first chapter of this book.

In 1988, I had a letter from Kenneth Holditch, whom I knew slightly, telling me that he was at work on a biography of Ken and asking me for my help. Because I knew he had good credentials, I let him have copies of my essay and copies of the letters that Ken had written to me. We have stayed loosely in touch through the years, for many of which his biography of Ken seems to have been placed on a back burner while he has published important works on Tennessee Williams, William Faulkner, George Washington Cable, and other major southern writers.

A year later, Barbara McIntosh, who had recently received a $100,000 advance from Harcourt, Brace, Jovanovich to write Ken's biography, wrote to me asking for my help with the project. I also shared my material with Ms. McIntosh, and spoke to her at length about Ken.

Years went by and I heard nothing more from her. In 1999, when I was working on this memoir, I tried to get in touch with her, but she was not at any of the several addresses she had given me, was untraceable even on the Internet. I wrote to Harcourt Trade Publishers, which was all that was left of Harcourt, Brace, Jovanovich, asking if they knew her whereabouts and if they still intended to publish her biography. I received a reply saying that Harcourt was not going to bring out the book and they had no idea what had happened to Ms. McIntosh.

In 1994, I received a letter from Deborah Hardy asking me for help with the book she and Rene Pol Nevils were writing about Ken. Her letter was accompanied by one from Les Phillabaum, Director of LSU Press, stating that Ms. Hardy and Ms. Nevils were writing the book under contract with LSU Press. "We would appreciate any assistance you can provide these authors," Phillabaum wrote me. Because of his letter, I assumed that their book was going to be a serious, scholarly work, and I was happy to oblige. I sent Ms. Hardy my unpublished essay about Ken and copies of the letters he had written me.

Subsequent letters from Ms. Hardy about the project aroused my suspicions. I thought some of her ideas for the book were bizarre. In one letter she asked for a photocopy of one of Ken's hand-written letters to show to a handwriting analyst in Baton Rouge in hopes of discovering something about Ken's personality. I am embarrassed to say that I sent her the sample she requested, thinking at the time that what she wanted to do with it was not something a serious biographer would consider.

In the last letter I received from Ms. Hardy, she wrote, in prose that did not inspire confidence: "It is only recently that the purpose of this book occurred to me, fell into my presence of thought, and that is we are writing this in order to free Ken's spirit." Perhaps, I thought, they should just have a séance instead!

Time passed and I heard no more from Ms. Hardy and Ms. Nevils. I thought that their book idea had probably mercifully died, only to discover in the spring of 2000 that it had not when LSU Press announced the forthcoming publication of *Ignatius Rising.*

LSU Press gave Carmine Palumbo a copy of the galleys of *Ignatius Rising,* which he shared with me. We both found it an appalling piece of work. I felt obliged to send relevant pages of the galleys to Nicholas Polites. I had put the authors in touch with Nicholas, and he was a primary source of their information about Ken. Nicholas was horrified when he saw what Ms. Nevils and Ms. Hardy had done with the material he had supplied. He wrote to Maureen

Hewitt, editor-in-chief of LSU Press, complaining that "so much of the information I provided has been embellished, distorted, and outright fabricated." LSU Press did respond to his letter and corrected some of the most glaring errors, but Nicholas realized that the book was irredeemably flawed. His letter continued:

> Please allow me to say that, to the best of my recollection, these pages strike me as one of the most unprofessional pieces of writing I've seen in some 35 years of a publishing, editing, writing and communications consulting career. That the text can be improved goes without saying. It has nowhere to go but up. Whether a halfway decent book can be made of it is another matter. The problem (aside from the brainless chatterbox style in which it is written) is that the writers have demonstrated their irresponsibility not only by inflating, but by distorting, taking quotes out of context, and putting words into people's mouths.
>
> With regard to parts of the text I haven't seen, I suspect that even if some things can be cleaned up, there's no telling where else in the text the writers have substituted factoids for facts and otherwise embellished on people's memories. . . . Unfortunately, because the book will be published by a university press, these factoids will be footnoted in subsequent scholarly publications and cited as facts. It will take a long time if ever to eradicate them.

I did not give the authors permission to use my essay, but they used it anyway, distorting it and paraphrasing it in very clumsy prose. I cannot complain too much about this for I realize I have only myself to blame for what a friend termed my "foolish generosity" in showing them my essay and Ken's letters. My attempts to keep them from using my material in their book met with no success. After corresponding with LSU Press about this matter, I thought that an editor was removing my material from the book, but she only took it out of direct quotation. Much of my essay was used and it appears without attribution.

The authors and LSU Press were also very high-handed in their dealings with Robert Gottlieb, who, when an editor at Simon and Schuster, played such an important part in the story of *Confederacy*. A publisher's note in *Ignatius Rising* acknowledges that Gottlieb's letters were used in the book without his permission, and that their inclusion constituted a failure to comply with the requirements of Fair Use. In a note to me, Gottlieb wrote that LSU Press "behaved with unbelievable arrogance and unprofessionalism . . . I could easily have stopped publication of their book, but didn't want to give it publicity."

I feel I was betrayed by Ms. Hardy, Ms. Nevils, and LSU Press, but the way I was treated is a minor offense when compared to the injustice they have perpetrated on Ken.

For reasons known only to themselves, the authors were over-eager to depict Ken as a homosexual, which he may or may not have been. They were unable to find any credible evidence for Ken's homosexuality, but did manage to unearth an unreliable witness with an unbelievable story of a sexual encounter he claims to have had with Ken. Someone named Chuck Layton told the authors that he had met Ken during the summer of 1967. At the time, Layton was a student at Tulane and had a severe drinking problem, and his "days and nights were planned around the acquisition and consumption of scotch." In spite of the fact that "many of the memories of sixties and seventies are a blur to him," when he saw Ken's picture on the book jacket of *Confederacy,* he claimed he immediately recognized him as a person he had picked up twelve years earlier in a French Quarter gay bar.

Given the way Layton described himself and the situation he was in when he claimed to have met Ken, the authors should have pegged him immediately as a highly unreliable source, probably someone trying to acquire a bit of glamor by associating himself with a celebrity. By including in their book Layton's far-fetched, unverifiable, and slanderous gossip, they have done Toole an enormous disservice.

All of the publicity I have seen which LSU has put out about the book mentions Ken's alleged "promiscuity" as if it were a well-established fact. In trumpeting it, they seem to have taken a page from the marketing technique of supermarket scandal sheets.

There are many other irritating elements in this book. Throughout the text the authors have inserted things that obviously they have only imagined.

To choose but one example, writing of the time Ken spent alone in his Lafayette apartment: "Ken did not encourage visitors and spent many hours alone reading, marking papers, and perfecting his party patter." I cannot believe that Ken ever spent time alone "perfecting his party patter." His brilliant wit was such that it did not need solitary rehearsing, but even if it did, only the cockroaches on the wall could have known what Ken did when he was alone.

Thelma Toole was an easy target for the writers. Thelma was a difficult and complex personality, but the authors have brought neither comprehension nor compassion to their treatment of her, and portray her as a two dimensional grotesque, almost a cartoon character.

Much of the information they give about her is inaccurate. Of her education they write that "Throughout her life, Thelma Toole gave the impression that she had been denied higher education because of her gender . . . " Never in the years that I knew her and listened to her tell the story of her life did she ever mention this to me. Since there are no footnotes in the book, it is impossible to tell where the authors got this bit of information. Did they just make it up because it sounded as if it might be true?

The authors write that she attended Soulé College, a commercial college where she received the certification which permitted her to teach in the New Orleans public school system, but they make no mention of the most important part of her education, the years she spent at the New Orleans College of Oratory and Dramatic Art from which she graduated at the age of seventeen. This institution was no doubt the most formative part of her education and explains a great deal about how she became who she was.

Kevin Allman, in his review of *Ignatius Rising* for the *Washington Post* (August 5, 2001), wrote that he found it "a puzzling book, and perhaps most puzzling of all is why LSU Press—where *Confederacy* is the eternal diadem in the catalog—would choose to publish such a sloppy portrait of their pet writer."

If I knew less about the story I would be more convinced

by this telling of it, but I can see that much of the information it contains is tainted, false, distorted, and that disturbs me. My view of the book is also colored by the anger and sadness I feel because the authors have so carelessly written half-truths and untruths about a friend who is not here to defend himself.

Letters from Ken

Here are the complete texts of the eight letters I received from Ken during a correspondence that began in early 1961 while Ken was in New York and I was in California. I gave the originals of the first two letters to Thelma and they are now in the Toole archive at Tulane. The remaining six letters came from a trunk I left in Florence when I returned to the United States in 1975. I retrieved them in the mid-1980s, and they are still in my possession. Where I have deemed it necessary, I have added explanatory notes at the end of each letter.

1) A hand-written letter on stationery with the letterhead of "Hunter College of the City of New York"
Dated: 2/3/61

Dear Joel,

Thanks for the Christmas card - including the brief note on your Mexican trip. The worst winter in 80 years has struck N. Y., and in my present snowbound condition find that letter writing alleviates some of the distress and discomfort of the below-zero temperatures.

I am currently nearing the end of a three-week vacation from both Columbia and Hunter—a vacation in which I accomplished none of the work I had intended doing.

As time passes, the tedium of graduate school magnifies; the Ph.D. looks like a nebulous and questionable reward for financial scrimping, stultifying research, and meaningless seminars. However, I like Hunter—principally because the aggressive, pseudo-intellectual, "liberal" girl students are continuously amusing. And the Hunter hierarchy has been more than kind toward me.

At this early date it looks as if Kennedy may justify my faith in him, although I'm only very grateful that we were spared Dick and Pat. What a disappointment the election must have been to Mrs. Montgomery! The WASPS were routed—in a sense.

During the Christmas holiday I was in N. O. and had an opportunity to visit Lafayette—and, surprisingly, I had a wonderful time. I was only there for a day, and this brief visit seemed to be the key to success: Lafayette is a nice place to visit, but . . . I also saw Nicky Polites—who was in N. O. on leave from the Army. Army life seemed to be depressing him, but fortunately he has received an early discharged to teach in some college in the Chicago area. But perhaps you know of this.

My best wishes to you. If you have occasion to see Gladys Waldron, please give her my warmest regards. I envy your moderate weather in San Francisco.

Sincerely, Ken

Note: Gladys Waldron was a dynamic and popular history teacher at Tulane. Although Ken and I had not known each other while we were undergraduates at Tulane, we both had taken courses with Dr. Waldron and had become friendly with her. In summer of 1957, after my graduation from Tulane, I had driven from Louisiana to California with her. I was going to California to report for duty as a freshly minted R.OT.C. ensign on the aircraft carrier U.S.S. Bennington. Gladys was escaping a painful divorce in New Orleans by spending the summer doing post-doctoral work at the University of California in Berkeley. Instead of returning to New Orleans, she accepted a teaching position at San Jose State College, and we kept in touch through the years until her early death from cancer in the late 1960s.

2) A hand-written letter on plain stationery.
Dated: July 9, 1961

> Dear Joel,
> Thanks for the invitation to visit—but this summer I'm finally getting around to doing the writing I've postponed for so long. Whatever comes of the creative endeavor, I will now at least be able to say I've tried.
> I should, I imagine, go to Lafayette some time this summer, but the prospect of Four Corners and College Road in all their heat and dust aren't too attractive. Anna Belle is asking for me—I may have to answer the call.
> The picture of Elizabeth [sic] was a thoughtful enclosure in the letter and was a fine illustration for your message.
> If you see Gladys, give her my best.
> Sincerely, Ken

Note: Anna Belle Dupuis-Hoffman-Krewitz was a colorful character in the town of Breaux-Bridge, near Lafayette. Ken had been introduced to her by his colleague on the USL English faculty, J.C. Broussard, who was a native of Breaux Bridge. Anna-Belle was a retired school teacher who held a kind of al fresco salon for her friends in her *Jardin d'une Soeur* (Garden of One Sister), a name inspired by the celebrated New Orleans restaurant, the Garden of Two Sisters. Anna Belle was very active in the promotion of French as a second language in Louisiana and one of the highlights of her life was meeting and being photographed with General Charles de Gaulle when he visited Louisiana in the early 1960s. After her late-in-life marriage to Roy Krewitz, an engineer who had for years rented a room from Anna Belle during the cane grinding season when he worked at a near-by sugar refinery, she enjoyed describing herself as "the most hyphenated woman in Louisiana." Like Ken's landlady, Elisabeth Montgomery, Anna Belle often wore a flower in her hair. The hibiscus was her blossom of choice. Mrs. Montgomery usually wore less exotic blooms, most often a camellia.

"The picture of Elisabeth" Ken thanks me for, was, of course, of Elisabeth Montgomery, and was probably from a newspaper article about Elisabeth's involvement in Lafayette's social scene as reported in The Lafayette Daily Advertiser. Since I was living in California when I sent the picture to Ken, I assume it was something my mother had sent me from Lafayette.

3) A hand-written letter on plain stationery
Inscribed: "San Juan, Puerto Rico/ 23 September 1962"

Dear Joel,

So Florence has claimed you for a while. I'm sure you could not have settled in a more ideal place; I can only discuss your good fortune with a mingling of envy and disgust.

We are all rotting here at the moment. The decreased draft has meant no trainees since June; therefore, there is no English to teach, and cobwebs and mold are beginning to overtake the SPEAK ENGLISH signs posted throughout the Training Center. I am now in charge of the English program here . . . a hollow position for the nonce. The benefits of the position are two-fold: supervision rather than teaching; a bright, comfortable, airy private room. The inactivity here, coupled with the remnants of a rainy and enervating summer has (have?) plunged the English instructors into an abyss of drinking and inertia. Occasionally someone will struggle off to the beach or to San Juan, but the maxim here remains, "It's too hot." Cafard, Bobby Byrne's nemesis, has struck. However, with the coming of winter, Puerto Rico weather is delightful, and the influx of tourists will once again revitalize San Juan. Our only project momentarily is to attend and destroy a production of Macbeth that an amateur group is staging on the ramparts of an old Spanish Colonial fort overlooking the Atlantic. One of the instructors is in the play—thus the general interest in the play's failure. We are to begin with cocktails early in the afternoon . . . and much later to proceed to the fort in a fleet of air-conditioned taxis. And so, with such plans, we pass the time . . .

The zenith of my summer was a trip to the Dutch island, Aruba, near the Venezuelan coast. A completely arid desert island, prehistoric in appearance, it is the perfect place for the proverbial moment of truth. And its starkness was an antidote for the overwhelming lushness of Puerto Rico. The bar at the resort hotel deserves great praise, too.

I found your letter here yesterday after returning from temporary duty at a SAC Air Force Base on the coast overlooking the Dominican Republic. The Antilles Command sent ten soldiers there for a tour/briefing of missile, etc. facilities. I still know nothing about nuclear warfare, but the terrifying destructive power of the things we saw combined with the disquietingly spirited manner of the proprietors of the missiles and jet bombers gave pause even to my desensitized tropical psyche.

I should leave Puerto Rico and the Army sometime next summer—barring a complete paranoid breakdown on the part of Fidel Castro. Please remit air fare via Pan American from San Juan to Italy. We now have direct flights to Europe. Any travel agent can handle the matter. You must be coining money at the American Language Center; with a title like that, the institution is obviously a front for something very lucrative and illegal.

Sincerely, Ken

Note: The American Language Center was an American-owned language school in Florence where I first found a teaching job that permitted me to remain in Florence. Later, a friend, Carl Selph, and I purchased the ALC's main competition in Florence, the American School of Languages, whose owners, an American man and his Italian wife, had got fed up, were on the brink of failure, and were moving to Los Angeles.

4) A hand-written letter on a lined sheet
Inscribed: "San Juan, Puerto Rico/ 29 November 1962"

Dear Joel

Since my correspondence (outgoing) has dropped to a virtual zero, I am once again beginning to wonder what the people I know are doing in their various situations. The arrival of trainees in late October has kept me very busy; as the "dean" of the English program here, I am lost in test scores and averages and in the maze of painfully intricate Army politics and intrigue. I am quite powerful in my own little way and exercise more control over personnel and affairs in general than I had ever suspected I would; over my private telephone I contact headquarters, switching people here and there, waiting, listening, planning. I'm sure I will leave my duty here a completely mad tyrant whose niche in civilian life will be non-existent. In its own lunatic way, this is very entertaining. I also enjoy posting edicts on bulletin boards; the last paragraph of my most recent proclamation reads:

"Further action will be taken against habitual violators of these regulations."

Early winter in Florence must be a contrast to my palm-and-ocean setting. The somewhat dubious organization for which you are working still, I assume, defrauds many gullible Italians annually. Your description of the faculty was what I more or less expected—a cross-section of American flotsam and jetsam. It is somewhat akin to the collection of drafted American wrecks teaching English here in the Training Center . . . although our disparate group finds a common bond in liquor.

After a year in Puerto Rico (as of 25 Nov), I find that the positive aspects of that year outweigh the negative. Although this seems a great cliché, I can say that I have learned a vast amount about humans and their nature—information which I would have enjoyed having earlier. In my own curious way I have risen "meteorically" in the Army without having ever been a decent prospect for the military life; but I feel that my very peculiar assignment has been responsible. The insanity and unreality of Puerto Rico itself has been interesting at all times that it was not overwhelming.

Please write. Ken

5) A hand-written letter on plain stationery
Inscribed: "San Juan, Puerto Rico"
26 January 1963

Dear Joel,

Back to the Caribbean again after New Orleans and all that it stands for. My holidays were very pleasant and very relaxing and, physically, New Orleans looked wonderful, as it always does. It is certainly one of the most beautiful cities in the world, although how the people who live there managed to make it so remains a mystery to me.

Repeated invitations from Lafayette and vicinity failed to lodge me from the comforts of home. However, Lafayette came to New Orleans in the form of J.C. and

Lottie Ziegler. I spent a few hours with them and "the Dutch couple" at the Roosevelt bar. The Dutch were quite pleasant, wise, and politic in the face of J.C.'s enthusiasms and Lotties's twitchings. Also present was N. Polites who contributed a few of the extravagances for which he is famous and which effectively silence tables for a few minutes while everyone stares at the floor. We must have appeared a dubious group in the bar, and I'm afraid that I made my departure rather rapidly . . . before the house detective took us all away. Polites is still spreading his own peculiar brand of fatalistic gloom as he continues to be thrust upon the thorns of life and continues to bleed quite articulately. Although I saw him only briefly during the holidays, he quickly and efficiently categorized the horrors of Chicago, New Orleans, and life. The robust positivism of Mario and of his mother are hilarious counterpoints to his breathy futility and negativism, and I was fortunate to visit with all three one Sunday afternoon. I also paid the ritualistic visits to the Byrne home (coffee, Aunt May, Mama, et al) where, of course, little has changed but the pot of fresh coffee and chicory. Bobby's worldview weathers humanity's derision and apathy. He does, however, begin to appear old. Both he and his brother received holiday visitors in long nightshirts and slippers with rather haughty formality, and Bobby was, as always, good for a dogma or two.

With Spring on the way, Florence should begin blossoming soon. At any rate, let me hear from you. Best wishes, Ken

Note: In late January of 1963, living in Florence, I received letters from Ken, J.C. Broussard, and Nick Polites, each describing an afternoon they had spent together in the bar of the Roosevelt Hotel (now the Fairmont) in New Orleans. Ken's was the funniest and wickedest of what I referred to as the "Roosevelt Hotel Triptych." Nick's letter described Ken as "developing his tendency toward inertia to a point of absolute self-realization." J.C. wrote: "Ken, so enwrapped in his own ego, responds and vibrates to one string which an acquaintance must pluck continually—his almost pathetic desire for being admired, his only conversation being his award for "best soldier of the month," the letters that Wieler from Hunter writes him imploring his return there, and the response I wrung from him by telling of former colleagues' desires to see him."

Lottie Ziegler was a professor of French at Lafayette, a family friend, and a very dear friend of mine. She apparently suffered from a mild form of Tourette's Syndrome that manifested itself in occasional facial tics. In spite of her German name, which she got from a husband to whom she was very briefly married early in life, she came from a prominent Louisiana French Creole family, the Montaguts, who owned a number of sugar plantations outside New Orleans.

In the summer of 1962, J.C., Lottie, and I had traveled together to Europe on the *Nieuw Amsterdam.* On board we had met and spent a good bit of time with a Dutch couple. J.C. was particularly taken with Olga, the wife, who reminded him of his idol Greta Garbo. They remained in touch and in January of the following year, the Dutch couple had made a trip to Louisiana to see J.C. and Lottie.

"Mario" is Nick's aunt, Mario Mamalakis, a woman in spite of the spelling of her first name, and the sister of his mother, Eugenia. Mario was for many years a teacher and librarian at USL. She eventually became the director of public relations, and, because of her competence and knowledge of university politics, emerged as a real power in the university hierarchy.

6) A hand-written letter on plain stationery
Inscribed: "San Juan, Puerto Rico, 9 February 1963"

Dear Joel,

A fairly cool period here seems to have succumbed to Puerto Rico's traditional warmth. Today has been warm, sunny, completely enervating. I ended the afternoon with several rums with lemon and water and lay beneath my mosquito net to contemplate the universe and my position in it. The results of this contemplation were negligible at best. An unusually gruelling (sp?) week here has left me totally suspended. Monday and Tuesday General McDaniel, the Inspector General of the Department of the Army, was here to inspect the English classes under my supervision; therefore, those two days were spent with a formidable array of brass. Staff cars converged on my area spewing out officers of every rank. Thursday morning we had to run through the Physical Combat Proficiency Course (a semi-annual hand grenade, horizontal bars, low crawl version of the Olympics). I went on sick call that morning. This morning we had to get up at 5:39 a.m. to go to mandatory breakfast in order to swell the numbers of breakfast eaters in our Company. None of the English instructors get up early enough to eat breakfast, and an attempt is being made to consolidate our mess hall with another as part of "Operation Stretch," a local Army campaign to save money. The instructors were so dead at breakfast that they couldn't find the corn flakes rack, etc. I don't like to bore you with this petty military information, but this has been the substance of the past week.

You were in an enviable position as receiver of the varying versions of the meeting at the Roosevelt. I wish that I had access to the other accounts, but it might be wiser to avoid the knowledge of the other revelations.

Last weekend I spent in Ponce, a lovely town on the south coast. The resort hotel there, the Ponce International, is built on a mountain overlooking the Caribbean and is certainly one of the finest and most relaxing establishments in the world. Fine bar, excellent and conscientious bartender. It was a very detached weekend.

I may have an opportunity to go to Ft. Jackson, S.C. for two weeks to set up and English program for Cubans there. I hope so.   Ken

7) A type-written letter on plain stationery
Undated, inscribed "New Orleans"

Dear Joel,

According to the itinerary on the postcard I received a while ago, you are once more safely in Florence. However, your seemingly inexhaustible supply of money may have propelled you elsewhere. Are you earning these travel funds at the American Center of Linguistic Superiority? Is someone interested in culture acting as your sponsor or patron? This needs explaining, I feel, for it is very discouraging to receive postcards from England containing vague references to Yugoslavia and Greece, especially when the recipient is in southern Louisiana at the time.

I left Puerto Rico in August. The two years in the Caribbean were, surprisingly, worthwhile from several points of view. I at least completed the active military obligation, and the Army treated me well (Remember that we are speaking here in the context of military treatment.) and gave me the leisure to accomplish several projects of my own. Puerto Rico itself was worth experiencing: one can appreciate Conrad much more deeply after having lived there for two years.

For now I have sought temporary shelter in New Orleans by teaching at Dominican College for the 1963-64 academic year. Because I teach only 10½ hours a week, I will seem to have the same leisure I enjoyed in the Army. The college has been in session for about two weeks, and so far the routine there has been extremely pleasant. Barring some Inquisition, I should have a serene year, and, with the salary they've given me, a very financially solvent one, also.

Aside from a brief visit with B. Byrne toward the end of the summer, I have had no connections with the Lafayette axis. According to Bobby, a meeting concerning textbooks held for the members of the English dept. late last Spring ended very badly indeed. Although he would not elaborate, he hinted that the meeting was climaxed by insults and near-violence. He did say that the Rickels were unwise enough to reveal their "total ignorance" at the meeting. Mary, I imagine, emerged

unscathed like some sort of USL Macmillan. But Bobby
was still (and this was in late August) extremely upset.
Very best wishes. Ken

Note: The "Rickels" are Pat and Milton Rickels, a couple
on the USL English faculty who were probably Ken's closest friends in Lafayette. "Mary" is Mary Dichmann, the
head of the English Department. "Macmillan" is, of course,
Harold Macmillan, the aristocratic Prime Minister of Great
Britain. The reference to Mary emerging "unscathed like
some sort of USL Macmillan" helps place the undated letter sometime before October of 1963 when Macmillan, far
from being unscathed by the Profumo affair, was at last
forced to resign as Prime Minister because of the sex scandal which had broken the previous summer.

8) A type-written letter on plain stationery
Dated 4 May 1965

Dear Nicky and Joel,
I know that you've been anxiously waiting this
letter for many months. What prompted my writing you was a visit from Viva Periou, who is in
town for a bankers' convention, last night. In the
course of our conversation which, naturally, evoked
all of the warm and happy memories of Lafayette
which I nourish greedily in an abandoned and rotting area of my psyche, Viva said that she had heard
that "Mr. Fletcher bought Joel a college in
Florence!" She was impressed—and, of course, I
was. In an epoch in which Ford Mustangs and

portable TV sets pass as gifts, a college is indeed a particularly large but also recherché gift. Bobby Byrne, who has been wanting a college of his own for many years, did not mention this to me the last time that I saw him; I suspect envy as the motivation for his silence. And in Florence, with the ghosts of the Guelphs and Ghibellines hovering, Bobby would be driven to new heights of teaching excellence.

Since both of you know of my writing project, I must say that eight air mail letters and one hour-long long distance call from Simon and Schuster later, I am still faced with revisions. Although I am "wildly funny often, funnier than almost anyone else around," the book is too "intelligent to be only a farce." It must have "purpose and meaning." However, it is full of "wonderfulnesses" and "excitements" and "glories." But they worked "more than three years on Catch-22." If and when it does appear, it will be unbearably "significant," I imagine. Also, I am like "one of those geniuses who turn up in Tanganyika or New Zealand." Poor New Orleans. Suppose I had sent the thing in from Breaux Bridge . . . or Parks. Broken and leering toothlessly, I may yet be on some book jacket. Looking at this more constructively, I have been (and am) fortunate in having the book reach so quickly people who have given me a degree of confidence in what I'm trying to do; goodness knows they've extended much time and interest.

All of which leads to something else, I guess. The Gulf Coast looks better when you're not there.

I was there recently; it looked much more appealing in undergraduate days. Even worse, I was in Alabama, too. Everywhere there are posters of Governor Wallace and every second car has a Confederate tag on its front bumper. All of this, I imagine, seems mercifully distant from your vantage points. Dominican continues to provide a substantial cushion for my assaults upon the world of literature. Although you may not agree, life here is certainly better that the masochism of living in New York, which has become the Inferno of America, the American Dream as Apocalypse. And I'd never be able to try to write anything if I were caught up in the Columbia-Hunter axis.

All of this pretentious babbling leads ultimately to a question: Are both (or either) of you going to be in New Orleans at any time during the summer? If so, let me know . . . and let me know what your plans are in general.

Sincerely, Ken

Sources

Ken and Thelma is based mostly on my own extensive archive of material about John Kennedy Toole and his mother, Thelma Ducoing Toole. My archive contains six letters and two copies of letters that Toole wrote me in the 1960s when he was writing *Confederacy of Dunces,* more than fifty letters and notes written to me in the 1980s by Mrs. Toole after the publication of her son's novel, and several hours of tape recorded conversations with her. It also includes copies of correspondence from Toole, Robert Gottlieb, and others, which were given to me by Mrs. Toole, letters to me from friends of Toole that mention him, my own journals from the 1960s and 1980s with entries about Toole and Mrs. Toole, and a large collection of newspaper and magazine articles about Toole, his mother, and the publication of *Confederacy of Dunces* and *The Neon Bible.* I also had access to the John Kennedy Toole archive in the Special Collections Division of Tulane University, which has many of Toole's papers, a bequest from Mrs. Toole.

I consulted as well the following published sources that contain useful and accurate information about my subject:

Coles, Robert. "Gravity and Grace in the Novel *A Confederacy of Dunces.*" The Flora Levy Lecture in the Humanities, 1981, Vol. II. Lafayette, Louisiana: the University of Southwestern Louisiana, 1983.

Griffin, Emilie. "Style and Zest: Remembering John Kennedy Toole." *Image: A Journal of the Arts & Religion.* 24 (Fall 1999).

Holditch, W. Kenneth. "Another Kind of Confederacy." *Literary New Orleans in the Modern World.* Ed. Richard S. Kennedy. Baton Rouge: Louisiana State University Press, 1998.

Palumbo, Carmine. "John Kennedy Toole and His Confederacy of Dunces." *Louisiana Folklore Miscellany.* Volume X, 1995.

Wonk, Dalt. "Odyssey Among Dunces: The Brief Life of John Kennedy Toole." *The (New Orleans) Times-Picayune.* Two parts: October 25, 1981, and November 1, 1981.

Index